Beyond the Present

Beyond the Present
A Memoir

Wendy Layne

Outskirts Press, Inc.
Denver, Colorado

The opinions expressed in this manuscript are solely the opinions of the author and do not represent the opinions or thoughts of the publisher. The author has represented and warranted full ownership and/or legal right to publish all the materials in this book.

Beyond the Present
A Memoir
All Rights Reserved.
Copyright © 2010 Wendy Layne
v2.0

Cover Photo © 2010 Wendy Layne. All rights reserved - used with permission.

This book may not be reproduced, transmitted, or stored in whole or in part by any means, including graphic, electronic, or mechanical without the express written consent of the publisher except in the case of brief quotations embodied in critical articles and reviews.

Outskirts Press, Inc.
http://www.outskirtspress.com

ISBN: 978-1-4327-5475-4

Outskirts Press and the "OP" logo are trademarks belonging to Outskirts Press, Inc.

PRINTED IN THE UNITED STATES OF AMERICA

Contents

About The Author i
Dedications And Thanks iii
Introduction v
CHAPTER 1: Alone 1
CHAPTER 2: Growing Up 15
CHAPTER 3: Lost Religion 27
CHAPTER 4: Back to Work 35
CHAPTER 5: Meeting A Stranger 45
CHAPTER 6: Music City 53
CHAPTER 7: Confrontation 65
CHAPTER 8: Lonely 71
CHAPTER 9: Selling The House 81
CHAPTER 10: Changes 89
CHAPTER 11: A Need To Know 101
CHAPTER 12: A Rainy Season 109
CHAPTER 13: Parties And Clubs 121
CHAPTER 14: Temporary Satisfaction 137
CHAPTER 15: A Symbol 147
CHAPTER 16: Moving To California 159
CHAPTER 17: A New Job 175
CHAPTER 18: A New Love 189
CHAPTER 19: Beyond The Present 211

About The Author

Wendy Layne was born in Midland, Texas in 1967. She was one of 11 children raised in a strict restorationist, millenarian, Christian denomination. She left her religion after her divorce and while she still considers herself a Christian, she prefers to remain denomination free. She sees herself as more spiritual than religious these days. Wendy believes in the "Live and Let Live" motto and embraces all types of people regardless of their religious beliefs. She has enjoyed writing from an early age and began writing poetry in her pre-teen years, keeping journals throughout her life. Wendy Layne is also an artist and although she works with various mediums she has a passion for watercolors. She is a computer enthusiast and loves all things electronic. She can't seem to have enough computers and has used all of them as yet another avenue to explore her creativity with website design, graphic design and audio and video creation. Wendy Layne is a big fan of the internet; Not only exploring but creating websites, blogs, e-commerce sites, and interacting in online virtual worlds. She loves all types of dancing and is currently enjoying learning ballroom dancing. Wendy is also an avid martial artist with experience in Chun Kuk Do, but describes the most fulfilling of all things that she loves as being a wife and mother and spending time with her family.

Dedications And Thanks

First and foremost, I'd like to dedicate this book to my children. The bond I have with my children is very special. Although the little ones are disappointed that they are not allowed to read my memoir until they are older, I have discussed my decision to write this book with my grown children and they know my purpose in writing it. I'd like to leave behind a legacy for my grandchildren and someday their children. After losing my dad, I have often thought of so many questions that I would ask him if I had another chance. There are so many things that I didn't know about him. And my younger sister Jennifer, who died when she was 19 years old and 8 months pregnant, what I wouldn't give to read just a page or two that she might have left behind about how excited she was to feel the little life growing inside of her, or her love for her husband Brian who was killed along with her in a tragic car accident. While this memoir merely covers a fraction of my life, it's a story that I am compelled to tell. It's a story that I want to be passed down so that future generations looking at my photos or my marriage licenses have not only the pictures and documents, but also the story to go along with them.

I'd like to say thank you to my mother. Mom, you have always supported me, stood back to let me make my own decisions, and had faith in a positive outcome. Thank you for not judging me, for being there for me, and for being the first person to truly love me.

I'd also like to thank my sister for being the one sibling that I could count on to be there for me. She is probably the only person that not only understands me, but also shares my history. She truly listened and showed unconditional love through all of my turmoil. We often speak of how we live parallel lives and how we share so many similar experiences, and if that is true, then it is her turn to find true, lasting love. Susan, I love you and no matter what happens with our relationships, I will always be your sister, your friend and confidant, and the person who will never judge you for your life decisions. I wish you love and happiness for as long as you live.

I'd like to thank my wonderful husband for showing me the meaning of true love. Thank you for supporting me through the process of writing this memoir. I know it has consumed a lot of my time and dominated many date night conversations. Thank you for being such a wonderful husband and loving father. Thank you for being my best friend. As we grow old together and build memories, we are bound to experience pain along the way, may we always see beyond the present. I totally, absolutely love you!

Last but not least, I would like to thank my editor, Angela Bickford, for her efficiency and all of her excellent guidance in helping me make this book a reality.

Introduction

This is not a work of journalism. The only claim that I make regarding interactions with people that are portrayed in this book is the recreation of my own emotions and memory. I have attempted to reconstruct my memories to the best of my ability; however, this memoir should not be held as a strict literal chronology of events. The quoted email exchanges or conversations are not actual word for word citations of the original conversations or emails, but have been recreated from my memory.

I recognize that by exposing certain facts about my own personal life I may be exposing facts about those that are, or have been, close to me. Therefore, I have changed the names of the actual characters, in order to maintain a margin of privacy. With all the characters names changed, it seemed only natural to change mine as well. Those who know me personally and choose to read my book will surely recognize some of the actual characters in my story. I urge readers to remember that each of these characters will likely have their own story based on their own memories.

My intentions for writing this memoir are merely as a method of healing and an avenue to reach out to others with similar experiences. It is not to harm or defame the character of others. Unfortunately, I cannot skip over pivotal events or pick and choose personal fragments of my life to omit and still tell my story in a way that makes emotional sense.

CHAPTER 1

Alone

Although his scent still remained on my pillow, the pain had been replaced with emptiness. As I lay in bed, the first morning rays of sunlight seeped through the cracks of my curtains. Although it had been almost a month since he left, this was the first morning I realized the changes in the little details of my life; the lack of conversation, the absence of his touch. I slid my feet off the bed and onto the floor and felt the carpet between my toes. Suddenly, my mind was flooded with memories of choosing this carpet with him. It seemed in everything around me there were memories of us, of when we were together. Now, I was alone.

    I stumbled down the hall to the kitchen for my morning dose of caffeine. As I opened the refrigerator, it was his drink and his favorite food that I saw. I closed the door and turned around, and as my back pressed against the cold refrigerator door, I slid to the floor. I could feel the tears in my eyes begin to form. The sadness and anger became mingled in my cluttered mind and I was not sure which emotion would win. It was as if his choice to leave me was worse than if he had died. Twelve years of marriage, three beautiful children, so much work, so much time invested. It was now broken. It had fallen apart. From the shattered pieces of my heart, to the broken dreams of my children, everything had changed. I wiped the tears from my cheeks and forced myself to my feet. The phone rang and my heart pounded with anticipation. I wanted it to be him, but I knew it wasn't. It was only my mother. We quietly exchanged greetings and she told me that the children were fine. The real thoughts were left unspoken. She knew that I would be fine because I was strong like her, but I knew she was also suffering and her heart was broken for me as my heart was broken for my children. I made arrangements to pick the children up on Monday because I was taking the weekend to gather some sense of what was left of my life.

On the opposite side of the dining room I could see my computer. The same computer we purchased together only a few months earlier. This was the computer that symbolized the beginning of the end. The end of everything we worked for, the end of all the promises made, and the end of our family as we knew it. I made my way across the room and sat at the computer, my hand gently resting on the mouse. Something was urging me to email her. I needed to let her know how I felt. She needed to know that she had contributed to the end of our relationship and disrupted the lives of our children. She needed to be aware that her actions affected a family and not just me. If I had only been a little less trusting. If I had only thought it could potentially be something more than just someone he met on the internet.

"Dear Angela, I don't know who you are and I know you don't know who I am. I am telling you this because you should know. You should know that I am a wife and a mother of three children, married for 12 years, and very much in love with my husband. But that's all changed now. My children are now a product of a broken home, a divorced family. I wonder if you feel that your encounter with my husband was worth the pain you have caused our family."

I signed the email with my real name, Madeline. Without a second thought I hit send. My inbox was filled with email. There was one particular email that caught my eye. It was from Robert. I met Robert the same time that Kyle met Angela. On the internet of course, the place where it all began, the deep, dark, secret world of chat! It was different for me. Kyle knew about Robert, but I knew nothing of Angela. And Robert knew I was married; I had no ill intentions. I was merely meeting new people and exploring the world of forums and computers for the first time. This was something we experienced together, a new kind of excitement and fun. As it turned out, it was a little more exciting and fun for Kyle than for me. All those late nights that Kyle would type on our computer came flooding back. He insisted I could not look over his shoulder because he felt uncomfortable with me watching him type, as if I would judge him for misspelling a word. He had never been good at spelling and of course, I believed him. I never imagined that the words he would type would mean sharing an intimate conversation with a stranger.

Email and chat were the avenues that allowed my husband to destroy our relationship, but in a weird, twisted way, it was now my place of comfort. It was a place where I could share with others my pain and frustration. I sat and shared with people who would listen, and possibly advise me, without any biases. They didn't know me, and I didn't know them. There was a sense of freedom in that type of relationship. I could share as I wished, and then with a press of a button they could be gone forever.

It was the same reason that Robert contacted me. He was looking for someone to listen to stories about his broken relationship and about how it had affected his daughter. Little did I realize that I would be in the same boat only a short time after meeting him. Now he was my confidant, a person to share my pain and cry with. He was someone who understood what I was going through. I opened his email. His writing style was eloquent and I could tell he was a well-educated man. This was a very vulnerable time in my life. I don't believe that Robert intended to take advantage of my weakness, but he did use it as an opportunity to invite me to join him far away from my small town and all of the pain that surrounded me. Although I had only chatted with and emailed

Robert, I felt comfortable and safe with him. There was one phone conversation I had with Robert while Kyle and I were still together. Because Robert was technically more skilled than we were, I took the opportunity to call him for technical assistance. Even with that telephone conversation I could sense his interest in me, though the feeling was not mutual. Now, I only felt pain and emptiness in my dull, aching heart. His email was shorter and more direct than in the past.

"I invite you to be my guest. It would be my pleasure to ease your mind during these difficult times. Your ticket is being mailed. Please accept."

I still felt no excitement while reading his email. I had no wish to meet him, and I was not sure what I would do. My heart was so full of pain that there was no room for reason, yet at the same time, there was no room for fear. I should have been afraid; I didn't even know this man, I only knew what he had written in his emails. But I was so overtaken with grief, and the grief was beginning to turn to anger. For a moment I entertained the thought, but decided to leave his email unanswered. Nashville, Tennessee seemed so far away from this little town in Texas. I wouldn't be able to tell anyone where I was going, who he was, or where I met him. No one would approve. Everyone would try to stop me.

I worked at a rehabilitation hospital and it had served to my advantage. Although the hospital was a physical rehabilitation facility, they had a resident psychologist available to help patients in their recovery. Dr. Wesley had become one of my best friends; sort of my own personal therapist without the charge or the official label that a person is given when they seek psychological help. When I was in his office he treated me as a patient, but in his eyes and in his voice, I could tell he really cared about me. I decided to tell him about my thoughts of leaving and visiting Robert. I didn't think I'd be able to be completely honest with him about where I met Robert, because he would be concerned for my safety, and rightly so. My mind drifted. I imagined what the meeting might be

ALONE

like, and then my mind snapped back to an earlier conversation with Kyle. It was a conversation in which I attempted to get all of the details of his encounter with Angela. I am not sure why I needed to know. I guess it is a woman thing. I needed to know if she was attractive, if she was smart, if she was better than I, and why he wanted her and not me. He wasn't able to answer many of my questions. Mostly he told me it didn't matter; however, he tried to lessen the experience by informing me that he was unable to complete the sexual encounter. As if his lack of orgasm would lessen my pain or my feeling of betrayal!

Although Kyle seemed to be expressing some form of repentance, his former religious conscience had been seared and I didn't feel he was asking for my forgiveness. And now as I sat there, contemplating accepting Robert's offer, I remembered that conversation with Kyle and his warning not to follow in his footsteps. I wondered what he expected from me. Did he honestly expect that I would remain celibate? Did he believe that he could leave me to follow his sexual urges and that I would never share another man's bed? I believe that although he wanted his freedom, like so many other men, he could not bear to think of another man caressing my body and making love to me as he had done so many times over the past 12 years. There had to be some sense of ownership or right to possession in his mind. My pain had begun to turn to anger and I felt a desire for revenge creeping into my soul. Thoughts of the age-old adage, "What is good for the goose, is good for the gander," begin to enter my mind. I felt almost driven to accept Robert's offer.

The house was empty and quiet. I should have been used to this feeling. Kyle was a firefighter and the house was often empty, but the emptiness felt different this time. It was as if the walls in our home knew that our family had been shattered. There was a stuffy, stale feeling in the air. I opened the dining room window and a gentle cool breeze blew across my face. The cold January air almost seemed to warm my frozen heart. As I gazed out the window, I was painfully aware of how every decision that I made could change my life as I knew it and everything that would happen in the future, just as the simple choice that Kyle made had drastically changed our lives. I was aware that every step that I took from there on out would have consequences. But at the same time, my world seemed to be spinning and I seemed to have lost control of what may or may not happen. I was not sure that I could trust my own decision-making process. Maybe I was experiencing a self-fulfilling prophecy. After all, in my father's own words, I had always been an optimistic pessimist, someone that was positive the negative would happen. I had to figure a way out of this thinking. I couldn't wallow in self-pity. There had to be a way to make positive changes in my life.

My day was half gone and I hadn't eaten. It seemed remembering to take care of simple necessities had become one of the most difficult tasks. My mother had become very important lately; my children were the biggest responsibility of my life, and in this state of mind I didn't feel capable of meeting their needs, but it was only temporary. School would start back on Monday and I had to pick the kids up the following evening. While I needed my space, I had to try and keep some consistency in their lives. It was difficult enough for them, and it was important for me to make sure that I didn't make drastic changes in their daily routines. As it stood, they would be coming home from school to a home without a father. We were accustomed to his 24-hour absence while he was away at the fire station, but his absence was now the permanent kind. Arrangements were made for Kyle to have visitation every other weekend. It was hard for me to believe that any parent could be satisfied with seeing their children every other weekend. I could only hope and pray that Kyle would become a larger part of our children's life than "every-other-weekend" as they grew older.

I decided to go out to eat. The house was filled with loneliness and my mind continued on its chaotic roller-coaster ride. I needed to be around people. I had always been a people person and I loved to watch them. Sometimes, I would sit in a crowded place and study how they'd come and go and often wondered what their lives were like. But now my thoughts were consumed with my own life and the tragedy that I was experiencing on what seemed like a daily basis. My eye caught a glimpse of the crayon marks on the wall as I slowly made my way down the hall to my bedroom. These were the marks made by my little son, and I traced them gently with my finger as I walked. Even this simple crayon mark flooded my mind with memories. I remembered how happy I was the day I discovered I would give birth to a little boy and how I rushed from the doctor's office to where Kyle worked to share the news. I remember that I wasn't sure if Kyle's excitement about our having a son was for the same reason as mine. I had wanted a baby boy for a very long time, and for me it was finally a dream come true. For Kyle, his mind could now rest. He knew that with this dream come true for me there would be no request for future children. We had agreed on this prior to conception and he wasted no time after Levi's birth having his vasectomy. I confess that I put pressure on Kyle for each of our children. I had such a burning desire to be a mother. It didn't really matter why Kyle was happy. I was so excited that we would have a son. The same little son that left his mark on our hallway with his crayons and whose little face had forever seared my heart with his expression when he discovered Daddy wasn't coming home anymore.

As I looked in my closet to decide what I would wear, I realized that the choices were limited only to what I wanted. I no longer had to take into consideration Kyle's feelings. I'm sure that would sound silly to the average woman, but Kyle was very possessive and was often upset by my clothing choices. It seemed ironic to me that one of the very things that elicited his attention before we were married became a cause for jealousy and anger afterwards.

I grabbed a pair of my tight jeans and a low cut sweater. The room was small and I only had to take a step backwards to sit on my bed. As I slid my satin nightgown over my shoulders and off my head, I caught a glimpse of my naked body in the mirror. Although my face looked tired from the stress and the tears, my body was in the best shape it had ever been in. At only 28 years, you would never guess that I had given birth to three children. As I slid my foot into my jeans, I felt the cold fabric squeeze my legs. The sweater was soft and was a gift from Kyle. I couldn't remember the occasion for the gift. Or maybe I chose not to remember. Maybe I felt that after I had touched everything at least one more time, I would stop remembering where they came from or the story behind them. It was as though all of my belongings were links of a chain, a chain that had now been broken into a thousand pieces.

    It was already one o'clock in the afternoon. I slipped on my shoes, gathered my jacket and purse, and headed towards the front of my house. As I left the house and locked the door behind me, I kept my head to the ground. The neighbors were not aware of my situation and I feared that they would ask me how Kyle was doing. I wasn't ready to share my story. I wasn't ready for more tears. The car was cold and took a few minutes to warm up. I tried to decide where to eat. It seemed strange to have lunch alone, but there were few friends left. Whether our former friends had taken sides with Kyle or me, or had not taken sides at all, the majority decided that I bore a scarlet letter: a "D" across my chest, a capital "D" for "divorced." In my state of depression, I had all but turned my back on my religion; however, my religious friends had turned their backs on me when I needed them most.

    I backed out of my driveway and headed towards a nearby restaurant. When I arrived, I felt as though I had left something behind, like my purse or my jacket. As I sat in the car staring out the window, I realized that this feeling would be staying with me for a while. This feeling was a close relative of loneliness; it was a feeling of being out of place and it was now clear to me why therapists always discouraged isolation during times of depression. I was not only alone I was also very lonely. There was a time when I longed to be alone if not for at least a moment. But that was back when the kids were bouncing off the walls and my life was crazy with the everyday hustle and bustle of raising children, making a living, and keeping a family functioning. But everything was calm for the moment. I was about to dine alone for the first time in a very long time, if not for the first time in my life. I wondered if this would be the beginning of many "alone" times and if I would adapt to these new sensations or if they would slowly drive me insane.

When I entered the restaurant a tall, thin, younger man approached me at the door.

"Will someone be joining you Ma'am?"

Under any other circumstance this would be a completely normal question, but it sounded different to me then, like he was saying, "Why are you alone?" or "What are you doing here without a date?" I sighed deeply before pronouncing that I would be dining alone. I tried to smile, but it came out crooked. I wondered if he could sense my discomfort. I studied the menu for what seemed like an unusually long time. Finally, the waiter approached my table.

"Ma'am, would you like to order or are you waiting for someone?"

Once again, I felt inadequate about dining alone.

"I'm ready to order. There will be no one joining me. I am alone."

My voice echoed in my head and I know I must have sounded rude, but he didn't seem to notice. My dining experience was less than satisfying. I found that I ate faster without company. The food tasted blander and my glass was never re-filled. Maybe the experience was typical. I chose to blame it on my lack of a dining partner, just as I chose to blame most of my negative experiences on my singleness, whether it be the way the receptionist treated me or the reason the officer gave me a ticket. No one seemed to feel sorry for me except me.

I spent the rest of my Saturday evening feeling my loneliness, not just being aware of its existence, but also truly contemplating the depth of my inner soul and the hollow area that had been carved from my chest when Kyle chose to sever our relationship. I knew that I could only indulge in my pain for a short time. Soon, I would be forced to face the reality of my new life as a single mother of three children. I tried hard not to ask myself that unbearable question, where upon considering the answer, I always end up wishing I could disappear. That nagging question; "Who would ever fall in love with a mother of three children?" I had heard all the statistics about how hard it was to find a husband after 30, and although I wasn't quite there, I was sure that the odds were against me since I could only see my children as a burden for any future relationship.

I quickly reminded myself that I was in no shape to be concerned about any future relationship and that I should only be thinking about picking up the broken pieces of my current life. I had no time for another man in my life. But still, men always seemed to come along and complicate things. It seemed like some men were expecting the breakup of my relationship, standing by patiently, waiting for their turn with me. The question remained to be answered whether or not I would give them a turn. I remember the many men throughout the years that could have easily been more than a mere temporary distraction had I not been so deeply in love with Kyle. Then there was Dr. Bernstein, a surgeon at the rehabilitation hospital I worked at. It was Dr. Bernstein who had almost ruined my relationship with Kyle only months earlier. Little did I know at the time that my marriage was already headed downhill.

Dr. Bernstein was a sophisticated doctor in his early 50's, however, his suave appearance and his obvious intelligence were somewhat waned by his speech impediment. He had a constant stutter; even more so when he was nervous. I suppose he was suffering from a midlife crisis and chose me to attempt to rejuvenate his once youthful inner self. He was always extra nice to me when visiting his patients. He'd make sure to stop by my desk, ask about my artwork, and pretend to be interested in something other than sex. I could see right through him, but I was obliged to treat him respectfully, and since he had never been forward enough for me to officially complain, I returned his niceties. One particular evening, Dr. Bernstein stopped by when I just happened to be working late. I could instantly tell his approach was a little different. His stutter was more prominent and he seemed extremely nervous. Most of the other employees had already gone home. Only the security guard was around. His name was Max and he was a good friend to me. I knew he had his own crush on me to deal with, but I was a few years older than he and married, and he had always been respectful of that. Max and I had been talking on speakerphone when Dr. Bernstein approached. Max was listening to our conversation, and I didn't bother to warn the doctor.

"I... I... I... ca... ca... can do a lot for you... you... you know? I... I... co... could make it where you'd nev... never have to... to work again."

"What makes you think I have to work?"

"Your... your... your... artwork... I... I... know people. You... you could be... a... a... successful artist."

Now, he was treading on sacred ground by making such remarks to imply that I could only be a success with his assistance.

"I don't need your money Dr. Bernstein. I will be successful without you."

It was clear from the moment I met Dr. Bernstein what he wanted from me. There was no need for him to be explicit now. We were not even on a first name basis and I was a bit shocked that he was being so forward.

"What about your wife Dr. Bernstein? What about her?"

"You... yo... you could... be... be my... Mistress."

Although I'd had many conversations with Dr. Bernstein in the past and I was familiar with his speech impediment, it was almost hysterical to listen to him stutter as he made his advances. I felt almost as if I were rejecting a little boy making his first attempt to score.

"You are offering to exchange money for sexual favors Dr. Bernstein. Somehow, I think you have mistaken me for a prostitute."

By the look upon his face I thought I saw a glimmer of guilt for a brief moment. Then he stammered for words to fill his next sentence.

"I... I... would... nev... never... think of... yo... you that way."

Interesting how he felt that his view of me made a difference.

"I'm not interested Dr. Bernstein, not at all. And just so you know, I will be successful someday, without your money or the people you know."

"I... I... I think you'll be s... s... sorry," he warned.

"I don't think so," I said as he turned to walk away.

I could still hear Max's breathing over the speakerphone. He had listened to the entire conversation.

"Wooooaa, did he just offer you money for sex?"

"I guess so, but I'm sure he'll leave me alone now. Surely he gets that I'm not interested."

But as it turned out, Dr. Bernstein did not know how to leave well enough alone. His persistence continued for weeks, and the calls became so frequent that it began to interfere with my job. Gifts and flowers would arrive, rejected of course. Eventually, after I realized he would not listen to my requests to be left alone, I approached the administrator of the hospital with my complaint. The administrator, Mr. Gregson, confronted Dr. Bernstein in a mild manner at first. This however, just angered Dr. Bernstein. His advancements soon became harassing threats. He told me that I should be careful. I was not really afraid of him, but was very annoyed that he felt he had the power to control me. Although I was fairly sure his threats were empty, I brought them to Mr. Gregson's attention. This time, the result was different. The following day, Mr. Gregson called me into his office.

"Maddie," he said, "I don't think he'll be bothering you anymore. Have you ever seen a man who stutters... really stutter?" He asked with a grin on his face.

"I think after I finished my "if he ever wanted to work in this hospital again" speech, it took him approximately five minutes to get another word out."

Mr. Gregson explained that Dr. Bernstein had previously had complaints filed against him for sexual harassment by other nursing staff.

I had never shared the details with Kyle. I knew that Kyle was already very jealous. According to Kyle, the clothes I wore or the friendly comments I made solicited the attention I received. He often accused me of inviting this type of attention. Of course, he referred to it as flirting, but I have never thought of myself as a flirtatious person. I am, however, very outgoing, and this was often mistaken as interest in the opposite sex when none existed.

It was only a few days after Mr. Gregson had spoken with Dr. Bernstein when Kyle stopped by the office. While we engaged in conversation, one of the female caseworkers, Anita, burst into my office unannounced and blurted out, "I heard about you and Dr. Bernstein." She turned to Kyle, "Have you heard about Dr. Bernstein's crush on Maddie? He's been showering her with gifts." Kyle looked my direction and I could see the shock in his face. He didn't have a clue what she was talking about. I had spared him the drama, or perhaps I spared myself, and now I appeared guilty. I knew that Kyle believed I was a flirt and that I enjoyed the attention I received. Even though my complaints were well documented, I knew there would be a fight. And of course, I was right. Once again, another uninvited man had complicated my life.

CHAPTER **2**

Growing Up

I grew up never knowing the word lonely. How could I possibly understand lonely coming from a family with 11 children. I didn't really know that our family was different, at least not in the beginning. By the time I was eight I had learned the meaning of poor. We were poor by most people's standards when you considered our financial status, but I never remember going hungry or being shoeless. With four older sisters and one younger, there was an abundance of clothes, and although they were mostly passed down from other families, they were new to us.

    I will never forget the first time I recognized that we had less than the average family. I had permission to spend the night with a friend from our church. She had only one brother and her own room, so needless to say I was very excited about visiting. What was interesting about the visit was that I don't remember what toys she had or what games we played. What I remember the most was the plush carpet on her bedroom floor and the flowery wallpaper on her wall. I remember the blanket on her twin canopy bed and the matching pink pillows. I remember sitting on her floor and pressing my fingers in between the soft, luxurious threads of carpet. Although this memory may seem insignificant, over the course of my life, it is this memory that would ultimately play a large role in shaping my hopes and dreams for the future.

BEYOND THE PRESENT

Her room was like something I had only seen on television. My room at home consisted of a concrete slab and barely framed in walls, exposed electrical outlets, leaks in the ceiling, and when it rained, water poured under the back door and flooded my room. It wasn't supposed to be that way. My father worked very hard to support us all, and he had built my room, which was an addition, with his own two hands. The rest of our house was much the same, in a run-down state with barely working appliances and an old gas stove to keep us warm at night. With our lack of resources, there were no shortage of people that felt sorry for us who would contribute food and other necessities. These friendly donations were mostly all I knew of gift giving, as my parent's religion was very strict and prohibited celebrating any holidays for fear of displeasing God by participating in traditions that took shape from a pagan origin.

In my very early childhood, I never really missed celebrating the holidays since everyone I knew was of the same religion and I was not allowed to watch TV programs that showed these celebrations. My only exposure to them was in school. It was quite awkward in the beginning as I remember opposition from an early age. Teachers would often get frustrated with my refusal to color a picture of Santa Claus, and I remember being called stupid by my kindergarten teacher. During birthday parties, I'd have to sit in a chair across the room and watch the celebration, unable to partake in the tasty treats, because eating them would be considered indulging in the forbidden birthday celebration. As time went on, it became easier and I learned to accept this non-participating way of life. I was taught that this would make me more like Jesus himself, as he said in the bible that he was no part of this world.

As I grew older my life became more complicated once again by my strict religious upbringing. As a teenager, it was difficult to make friends because I was so different. People often shun that which they do not understand. I was never allowed to spend the night with any friends unless they were of the same religion. My non-participating social life had become even more complicated in high school as I learned that competitive sports, running for school offices, and attending pep rallies were not allowed as they were considered preparation for a political like structure in the real world where my parents religion promoted a neutral political view, unable to vote or participate in political activities. They felt that once again, this is what Jesus would want since he was no part of this world.

Even school dances were not permitted since other children who were not part of our religion were considered to be bad association. I had begun to feel like I was no part of this world, no part of the school, with no friends. I felt like I had no real future or plans for a real life. The only plan really set before me was to marry and have children and teach my children the same religion that I had been taught. College was not an option for many reasons. First of all my parents could never afford it, and second; it was felt that by going to college I would be opening my mind to selfish ideas and developing a "me" attitude as opposed to being selfless and storing up treasures in heaven. I felt different, yet at this stage still not unhappy. With so many brothers and sisters, there was still much to keep me busy. And fortunately for me, as I entered the bloom of youth, there was at least one boy in our congregation that interested me.

His name was Kyle. I was 14 when we met and for me, although it was not love at first sight, it was instant infatuation. That word was one I would hear over and over again from my parents as I began to fall for Kyle. He was only 16 when we met, but he appeared much older. He was already 5' 10" and muscular, and since I was small and thin, he appeared manly to me. He had beautiful blue eyes that seemed to pierce my soul. He made me feel so much older than only 14 and he made me feel so beautiful. After spending time with him, I would look in the mirror and it was like a sudden transformation from an ugly duckling to a beautiful swan right before my eyes. I had never felt so beautiful in my life.

My father kept a careful eye on his many beautiful daughters. While many fathers would not trust young boys around their girls, my father never trusted his girls around young boys. My father was in his late forties when I was born and I had three younger siblings. With six girls and five boys, you would think minor transgressions would go unnoticed. But that was not the case. It was like there were spies following my every move and reporting directly to my father. Although I was a very good girl and very much afraid of displeasing my parents, I knew that I was no different than the other girls in the family. I was a liability. It was important that I shine as a good Christian. My father was an elder in our congregation, and just as 1 Timothy 3:7 stated, and he would constantly remind us, he had many standards to live up to if he was to continue as an overseer of our congregation. Those standards included presiding over his household in a fine manner and having children in subjection with all seriousness. If indeed any man does not know how to preside over his own household, how will he take care of God's congregation? I am sure that it was this scripture that contributed to my getting married three days prior to my 16th birthday.

Only a few months after meeting Kyle, it was all too obvious to my parents that I was headed down a dangerous path; a path laden with the sin of fornication. The only way to clear that path was to eliminate the sin. The only way to eliminate the sin was to marry before the act was committed and change the entire situation from a potentially sinful act that would be punished by excommunication, to a blessed and honorable arrangement by God. Nine months prior to my 16th birthday, Kyle and I were engaged and just as my parents wished, my virginity was maintained until my wedding night. Within seven months of our marriage I was pregnant with our first child. I conceived during the summer between my junior and senior year in high school and had decided that the best option was to drop out of high school and raise our baby girl.

Kyle and I spent the next 12 years happily married. Or so I thought. We became parents to another beautiful baby girl and five years later, a little boy. After three children and many ups and downs over our marriage, I remained devout to the only religion I had ever known; however, my life did not follow the same degree of strictness that my childhood had. Over the years my desire to do something more with my life had finally taken its toll, and I obtained a GED and enrolled in a continuing education course to become a secretary. While I was proud of my accomplishments and couldn't wait to advance to a new career, the more I learned and the brighter I got, the more jealous Kyle grew. He was never excited about me working outside the home. I understood his feelings because he had been raised the same as I had, and with that type of upbringing one thing was clear: a woman's place was in the home. But my place couldn't be in the home forever. I longed for a deeper satisfaction with life and I had so many talents that I was ready to share with this forbidden world that we had spent so many years remaining separate from.

Up to this point in my life, I had become my mother. Although I loved her dearly, and being a good wife and mother is surely virtuous, I was not living my dream, but merely living hers. I had begun to feel that I was meeting everyone else's needs while neglecting my own. Towards the end of our 11th year of marriage, I had expressed to Kyle my disillusion with our religion. I no longer had the faith that my religion was the true way to worship, and I shared this with him hoping to reach some part of him that would agree with me. Each time I discussed my feelings it seemed that it would drive a wedge between us. Yet all the while, I remained deeply in love with my husband.

Our life seemed to be peaceful with the exception of the occasional screaming matches that I had assumed were a given for even the happiest of marriages. Things had been going well for both Kyle and I. I continued to learn new skills and eventually obtained a job as a secretary. After a couple of years of applying at numerous fire departments throughout the country, Kyle eventually was hired locally and worked as a firefighter/paramedic.

It was not until our first major crisis that things started to fall apart. It was just after our 12th anniversary when our baby boy fell ill with chicken pox. It didn't seem unusual, since the girls had already recovered without any problems. But Levi was different. One of his open sores had apparently become infected and bacteria had traveled to his knee, causing what was described to us as osteomyelitis. Levi was barely three years old when he had surgery on his leg to clean the infection and was hospitalized for almost four weeks. His being in the hospital was incredibly difficult for us both. It was as if everything that could go wrong went wrong at the same time.

It was December, and while to the outside world December is a time for families to gather together, to celebrate, and to be merry, for our family this December was a stressful and chaotic time. We had adjusted our schedules so that the two of us could alternate being with Levi in the hospital and still continue to work at our jobs. It has been said that a couple that can weather a storm together will stay together. Kyle and I were not weathering the storm very well. It seemed that every conversation turned into a fight. Not only did our relationship seem to be failing us, everything around us seemed to be affected by this low spot in our life.

In addition to the concern and fear we had with Levi's condition, due to our overworked schedules and hectic lives trying to manage our two young daughters as well as our jobs, somehow we failed to pay our auto insurance on time. As Murphy's Law would have it, I was leaving the hospital one afternoon, and as I reached for the door handle on my car, I discovered that the door would not open. As I stepped back to take a second look, I realized the entire side of my car had been smashed by another vehicle. I felt like the world had come crashing down on me. What had we done so wrong to have such horrible luck at the worst possible time?

By the time Levi had come home from the hospital, things had started to mellow out. I was beginning to think that things would return to normal. Thanks to the insurance company feeling sorry for us in our time of need, they extended our auto insurance and covered my auto repair even though it had already lapsed. Levi was receiving in home nursing care for the daily antibiotics that were given to him intravenously. Things appeared to be on the up and up. But the serenity was short lived. Instead of fighting, Kyle had begun to drift away. It was as if he was giving me the silent treatment. I wasn't sure what I had done or what was going on in his head, but I knew something was different.

He'd be on the computer for hours late into the night, and when I'd enter the office to talk to him, he'd close his programs quickly. He would always tell me he'd join me in bed soon, but had to finish some things first. I knew he was spending a lot of time on chat. It had become a new form of entertainment for the both of us since I had saved enough money from my new job to purchase a new computer just a month earlier. But usually we spent time together on chat, and we both found it interesting that there were so many people; strangers that would all come together in this unique new forum to discuss everything under the sun. Some people would discuss politics, which was a subject that neither Kyle nor I had an easy time discussing due to our religiously neutral upbringing. Others were looking for cyber-sex, something we both found hilarious.

We had met many different people and we often wondered if any of them were really what they said they were. Some of our chat sessions proved to be very useful. I met a man who turned out to be an excellent source for technical support. I was just learning about computers, and although I was very interested, there was still so much I didn't understand. Being the mid '90s, I has very few friends that actually owned a computer. It was a fascinating new experience and I was eager to learn. I never worried about Kyle chatting late at night. I trusted him, and there was a sense of security chatting on this electronic box in our home where the people were so far away that the distance almost made them seem imaginary.

After 12 years together, our marriage had become such a constant in my life that I believed it was impenetrable by any outside threat. After all, my parents had done a wonderful job raising me to believe that we as a religious group were among the only people in the world that had faithful marriages and led true Christian lives. It was as if my religion was an automatic protection from any and all sinful tendencies. But what was about to unfold would shake the very foundation that I had been placed upon from infancy, the rock under my feet, and the strength in my soul.

It was Thursday night in early January, and as we slipped into bed for the night, Kyle turned away from me to face the wall and pulled the covers up to his chin. It was an unspoken message that he would not be engaging in idle conversation before sleep. Since Levi's illness, I had become used to the silent treatment. It had not always been this way. For most of our married life, our bed had been an unwinding place at the end of the day. It was our haven away from the rest of the world, a place to share the most intimate of secrets, and where we planned the exciting future that lay before us.

As we lay together in bed, I sensed that we were together but somehow separate. With emptiness in my heart from the distance I had begun to feel from Kyle and a longing for intimacy, I pulled myself up behind him and curled my body around his in an attempt to reach him in the one form of intimacy that I knew he had always been eager to share.

I gently whispered in his ear, "Do you want to make love?"

He responded, "I'm getting sick, I don't feel like it."

"You've been saying you are getting sick for a couple weeks now, are you really sick or are you avoiding me?"

"I'm not avoiding you, but we do need to talk".

I was excited at the prospect of conversation, as it had been lacking between us since Levi had gone to the hospital.

"So let's talk."

"I have to work tomorrow, let's talk on Saturday when I get home."

It was only Thursday and he would be leaving for the fire department on Friday morning and would be gone for 24 hours. I couldn't wait 24 hours to have a conversation that he said we "needed to have."

"I want to talk now."

He turned over and I slid back to my side of the bed. I was not sure what the conversation would be about and was eagerly awaiting his comments. Perhaps something was bothering him from work. He was a paramedic and oftentimes he'd experience some traumatic event. Perhaps he'd witnessed the death of a child or he'd comforted a dying man and promised to deliver his last wishes to his wife and children. There could have been any number of things bothering him, but I was sure it was nothing I had done.

"Ok, if you insist, we will talk."

The soft glow of the bathroom light reflected off his face as he began to speak, and I could see his facial expressions change. Suddenly, I had a feeling that something I didn't want to hear was about to be spoken from his lips.

"I have not been sick this week, not literally. I've been sick because I realize that I don't love you anymore."

My heart sunk. I was not sure I had heard him correctly. Maybe I was dreaming and I would wake up in a few minutes and laugh about how I'd had this horrible dream.

"WHAT? You can't be serious!! What do you mean you don't love me?"

Kyle rarely communicated his feelings. He was not much of a talker, yet on this night, he poured out his feelings as if they had been bottled up inside for a long time. Finally he could no longer contain them, and he began to overflow with words that flooded my heart with pain.

"I'm not in love with you," he said again. "I haven't loved you for a long time and it's just now to the point that I can't stand it anymore."

As he continued to deal the emotional blows, I sat up in the bed, still in some semi-conscious state of shock, until the emotion took over and the pain and hurt in my heart took on the form of anger in an attempt to protect my fragile psyche. I cried and screamed and we argued for what seemed like an eternity, but in reality was probably only 20 minutes. It seems surreal that a single 20-minute fight would be the end of a 12-year relationship. I couldn't believe it was actually over. It felt as though there was nothing left for me to say because Kyle had made up his mind. I couldn't bear the pain any longer and as Kyle packed his bags to leave, I wiped the tears away and realized if I had any chance to save our relationship, I needed to remove the kids from the house and convince Kyle to stay and try to work things out with me. I begged him to stay as I prepared to wake the kids and take them to Grandma's. I didn't want the kids to know that anything serious was happening, but I knew that the girls would suspect something because they had school the following day and I rarely kept them home. I managed to scoop the kids up as they remained in a semi-sleep state and place them in the car one at a time, all the while with Kyle telling me I didn't have to leave because he was leaving. I left home with the kids without warning my mother. When I arrived, I gave her very little information, although I knew that she knew something serious was unfolding. In all the years we had been married, I had never involved my mother in any of our conflicts, and this time I was leaving the kids for a sleepover in the middle of the night. My mother could see the pain on my face, and I could see the reflection of that pain when I looked her in the eyes before heading back home to Kyle.

As I drove back home, I felt an emptiness begin to invade my heart. I thought about the words that Kyle had spoken and how he claimed that he had fallen out of love with me. I had always craved his attention and often felt that my love for him was stronger than his love for me. If I ever brought up the subject, he would try to explain that he loved me to the ability that he could love. It was as though he experienced some abbreviated form of love, some type of love that was limited by his ability to show emotion. Kyle would chalk it up to a fundamental difference between men and women and somehow the entire issue would be turned around to point at me. Somehow, instead of being reassured of his love for me, I'd feel that I was suffering from my own inadequacies due to my lack of confidence and trust in our relationship. I had learned not to introduce the subject at all and instead turned to the only form of intimacy that Kyle seemed to be eager to share, the physical form. Over the past 12 years, sex had become the only way that I could truly feel loved by Kyle. I knew that sex couldn't save our marriage. I wondered if it was possible that Kyle had truly fallen out of love with me, or if maybe he had never really loved me at all.

When I arrived home, my heart sunk when I realized Kyle's car was gone. He had left and I had no idea where he had gone. Somehow, in my heart I knew that this was the beginning of the end and no amount of begging or pleading would convince him to come back to me. For the first time in my life, I felt truly alone.

CHAPTER 3

Lost Religion

I used to attend church on Sunday mornings. But now I was bitter and church was a place for families. I couldn't bear to bring myself to a place where Kyle still attended. The ministers of my church had advised against sharing details about our break-up with any of my friends in the congregation. They were concerned about the defamation of Kyle's character.

In the beginning, even my boss, who was of a different denomination, encouraged me to seek refuge from my pain within the church. I lived in what is considered the 'Bible Belt', and church was the answer to the majority of life's turmoil. Although I tried, my church was not a place of comfort for me. It seemed that the majority of the ministers in our congregation sided with Kyle, as the man of our house. Every piece of advice I was given seemed to go against the grain. Of course, in the beginning Kyle had not confessed his adultery. And even after the issue was raised and Kyle was actually reprimanded by the church, I was discouraged from seeking a divorce.

Most of the friends that I had made within our church turned out to be mere acquaintances and not true friends. When the going got rough, they bailed. My only true friend turned out to be the wife of Kyle's ambulance partner. Although Courtney and I were very different in many ways, we had a lot in common when it came to motherhood. Since our husbands were both firefighters and were away for 24 hours at a time, there were many opportunities for us to get together. It was Kyle who actually insisted on our meeting; however, all the credit would have to go to Courtney and her persistence, which eventually forged a close friendship between the two of us.

Courtney would often call just to say hello and ask what I was doing. I never was much of a phone person and eventually had to purchase a cordless phone just so that I could get my work done around the house without having to hang up on her. Mark, her husband, although he was very close to Kyle, could easily recognize the guilty party. He often told me how Kyle had become a different man than the one he had known for so many years. It was a good feeling to have Courtney and Mark remain my friends, but still, it was different now. Our relationship had always been a foursome and now it was awkward. I felt like a third wheel. Slowly our contact with one another began to lessen. And the more I withdrew into my shell, the less contact I wanted with anyone, especially anyone who was a part of our former life.

That Sunday morning, I had no reason to get out of bed at all. The kids were staying the night with my mother. There was no more church for me. No friends to call. I lay in bed, awake but half asleep. Most of my waking hours consisted of similar half awake, half asleep feelings. I seemed to be drifting without any direction.

I rolled over in bed and reached for the phone. I needed to hear the voices of my children. I had to make sure they were ok. Regardless of how much pain I was in and how much I knew they were in good hands with my mother, there was that burning inner part of me that, since I first became a mother, would not let me relax without checking on them periodically. I dialed my mother's phone number, and my oldest daughter Katy answered the phone.

"Hi Mom, I miss you!"

"I miss you too honey. Are you having fun at Grandmas?"

"Yeah, and Daddy called and said he is taking us to dinner tomorrow night!"

"Oh he did!"

I was surprised, but I shouldn't have been. Kyle rarely talked to me before making plans with the kids. He seemed to avoid any conversation with me lately. It was like the children were the communication line. I knew it wasn't healthy for them and they were often caught in the middle of things they should have never been involved in.

"Yeah, he said he's picking us up from Grandma's tomorrow and taking us to get a hamburger and ice cream and then he said he'd drop us off after you get home from work."

"Ok, honey, I'm happy for you guys. I'm sure you'll have fun."

I would never let her hear any disappointment in my voice. Although I was torn between the love I had for her father and the hate I had for what he had done to our lives, it was important that they love their father and not sense my anger. He was the only father they had and as painful as it was for me, it was important to make sure they knew that we both still loved them dearly. I spoke a few more minutes to Katy about how Grandma had been spoiling them, and then I said good morning to Kaleigh. I asked her to give a kiss to Levi for me since he was still sleeping, and then I gently hung up the phone.

Kaleigh was my little angel. She was only eight years old and so sensitive. It was like her pain was more for me than for herself, and although she constantly attempted to take care of me, I knew inside she was suffering silently. She would spend hours trying to help clean or put toys away and ask me if I needed anything. She never cried out loud and if I weren't her mother, I'd think she was unaffected by our divorce. But the more she tried to be a good little girl the more I could feel her pain inside my chest. I knew she felt that if she could just be better or do more that Daddy would come home again and we'd be a happy family. I worried most for little Kaleigh.

My little Levi was barely three and wasn't sure what was going on. All he knew was that Daddy now had an apartment and it was so difficult for him to transition back and forth. When he'd leave Kyle's, he'd cry to stay with Daddy and then when Kyle would pick him up again, he'd beg to stay with Mommy. My heart would ache for him each time we'd make the hand off. It was like he was being stretched between the two of us. I was saddened because I knew there would come a day when he didn't even remember living at home with both Mommy and Daddy. He was outspoken and I was thankful that most people couldn't understand his baby talk. He'd be in the basket at the grocery store and he'd tell the nice lady in the deli section that his Daddy left us. She'd have to ask me what he said and I'd stumble for words and try to be creative, "He said his Daddy loves him," and then I'd smile as I hurried on my way.

Katy was my strength. She was only 10 but seemed so mature. I believe our divorce was forcing her to grow up even faster. It was Katy who first suspected her father's intentions for leaving. Although he tried to say he had merely fallen out of love with me, and my story to the kids was that Daddy needed some time to be away from Mommy and that he still loved them dearly, she saw beyond our stories. From the beginning, I remember her tears and screams. She was very emotional and the most like me. She was the most outward of the children with her grief. I remember her crying and telling me that she knew Daddy must have a girlfriend because he would never leave me unless he loved someone else. She was such a smart little girl, yet I was blinded by my love for him and refused to accept the fact or see the signs that there was someone else.

As I lay in bed, I contemplated calling Kyle, but I felt sure that it would not be a pleasant conversation and I wasn't in the mood for confrontation. I was angry that he had not made arrangements with me to take the kids to dinner and I knew that if I called him right now I would not be able to contain my anger. I was beginning to believe that he did this type of thing just to irritate me, and it was probably better to just let sleeping dogs lie.

I slid out of bed and stumbled to the bathroom to brush my teeth. A few of Kyle's things still remained in the medicine cabinet next to my toothbrush. I was tired of seeing them every morning and I scooped them up and dropped them in the garbage can. I closed the medicine cabinet and gazed into the mirror at my reflection. Other than the tiny lines, which I referred to as smile wrinkles, my skin was very smooth. Although I was definitely not old at only 28 and I appeared very young, I had already experienced 12 years of marriage and 10 of parenting. I wondered when others looked at my eyes if they could see the pain behind them and if they'd ever guess that I had been through so much at such a young age. It seemed once again that I was absorbing more details in my everyday surroundings than I ever had before.

I finished my morning ritual and sat down at my computer. My inbox was empty except for another email from Robert waiting to be opened. He wanted to know if I would be flying to see him. I am not sure if it was my anger toward Kyle or just the boredom from my loneliness, but I replied to the email with the word "Yes," nothing more, nothing less, just "Yes." In either case, it was a diversion from the present circumstance none-the-less.

I knew that if I was going to do something so crazy that I needed to tell someone where I was going. I was not sure whom I could trust or how much I should tell. Although I was pretty sure Kyle did not want custody of the kids, I felt sure that if he found out that I was going to see Robert, he would use it as a way to prove that I was an unfit mother. But even if he did find out, I knew his priority would be how much child support he would have to pay, and I was sure that anything could be plea bargained.

There was only one person I could tell, and that was Dr. Wesley. I would have to be careful, because his job would be to stop me from going. I was a horrible liar, so I would have to try and stretch the truth. In as few words as possible, I'd have to stage it as if Robert and Lara were long time friends. Hopefully, Dr. Wesley would assume Lara was Robert's wife. I wasn't planning on telling him she was his daughter. I was not sure if Dr. Wesley would think it was a good idea, but if I convinced him that I needed this break and provided him with the address that I would be staying at, at least someone would know my whereabouts. Although I felt quite safe, I knew that my decision to meet Robert was foolhardy. Not very many people would make the same decision. This was a new age. The internet was brand new. It was all about chat. Most people were still afraid of it, so I would never mention to others that I was spending hours every evening communicating with people I'd never met in order to fill the void in my life. I was still amazed at how this small box that I brought home from the computer store could wreak so much havoc on my life. Yet I continued to invite these strangers into my home electronically. I was drawn towards the unknown and craved something new or better in my life. Everything seemed so bleak. After all, whatever it was that was out there was enough to take Kyle from his wife and three children. Maybe there was something for me.

My excursion was only a week away, so I spent the rest of Sunday pretending I was preparing for a routine vacation and gathered things that I would take with me. I had no plan for what type of visit this would be. I wasn't sure if I'd go out on the town, hang out at his house, take walks in the snow, or just cry on his shoulder, and it was difficult to prepare for the trip. I was still a little scared that I had made a bad decision, but something was driving me. I think there was a tiny portion of me, as unbelievable as it seems, that didn't really care what the outcome was. In my state of disillusion, if Robert turned out to be some psycho who killed me, I figured that Kyle would feel guilty and have to live with what he'd done. Of course, this was only a passing thought, and when my mind would drift back to my children, I'd realize that revenge was not worth dying for. It was then that I'd have a bit of fear enter my mind, but I refused to let my common sense win. I always had a rebellious nature and I remembered how my dad would say that someday, some poor guy who'd get his hands on me would realize he had a tiger by the tail. At this point, I was determined to visit Robert, although I couldn't exactly say why.

As my Sunday drew to a close, I felt that it was my last day of rest. Tomorrow I would return to work. As darkness fell, I crawled into my empty bed. I was cold and longed for companionship. I remembered the feeling of Kyle's strong embrace, and as I closed my eyes, one lone tear rolled across my cheek and landed on the soft cotton pillowslip. I brushed my hand across it as if to erase the evidence of my pain.

CHAPTER 4

Back To Work

I was lucky to work for such an understanding company. My immediate supervisor was Kay Marison, the Director of Nursing at the hospital, and her husband George was an Army chaplain. They had no children and it was as though Kay and George took in the employees of the hospital as their own surrogate children. They cared a lot about others and were always willing to lend a helping hand to anyone in need. I assumed that was the reason for their choice in careers.

Kay had been there for me from the moment that Kyle left. I remember how crazy I had been after staying up all night the Thursday evening he announced his position in our relationship. Although I had not slept a wink, I still showed up for work that Friday morning, but showed up is about all I did. My face was swollen and my eyes were blood-shot. I was like a zombie wandering the hall towards my office. When Kay found me, she immediately knew something was wrong. She had me go straight to Dr. Wesley's office, and I spent my working hours for the first two weeks after our separation there in his chair listening to his comforting words instead of performing my daily tasks. I was paid the same none-the-less.

Dr. Wesley's words were not always what I wanted to hear. He dealt a lot of harsh criticism, but it was mostly directed at the situation I ended up in. He seemed to blame my religion for my lack of confidence. He would constantly have to remind me that I was worth more than what I thought. He opened my eyes and helped me see that everything I had believed in was now different and that I had to re-shape my entire existence. For me, my young marriage seemed normal. For Dr. Wesley, it was absurd. He couldn't fathom how any parent would sign for his or her virgin daughter to be married at 15 years old. I believe it was partially his frustration with this issue that caused him to sort of take me under his wing. He wanted to help me and wanted to see things turn out well for me.

My daily sessions with Dr. Wesley had become weekly at this point. I felt like he was weaning me from his care. I was, however, becoming very attached to him. Often, I felt that my attachment was a little weird. Although Dr. Wesley was probably 20 years my elder, he was very handsome and there was something about his caring about me and his soft soothing words that attracted me to him. I knew he was married and although he was very professional, there was a relationship being built between us. I had heard of patients becoming abnormally dependent on their psychologist. I knew that I was vulnerable, and it was a good thing that Dr. Wesley was as professional as he was and never overstepped his boundaries. In my vulnerable state, I am not sure that I would have been able to stop any romantic advances on his part.

I had been avoiding Dr. Wesley because I was hiding something from him. I was typically very open with him because he was willing to hear my deepest secrets and seemed to understand me, if nothing else, from a medical viewpoint.

My day at work was almost over and I had to prepare to see Kyle that evening when he returned the kids after dinner. As I gathered last minute items together, I realized I needed to take some things to the nurse's station. I headed around the corner with an armful of papers and bumped smack into Dr. Marx. My papers fell to the ground and Dr. Marx bent down to help me gather them up. For a moment we looked into each other's eyes and his eyes seemed to almost glisten. His voice was deep, but soft.

"I'm sorry," he said.

"No, I'm sorry, I'm clumsy and distracted these days."

"Yeah, I heard you are going through a divorce?"

Dr. Marx was a little blunt. He'd gone through one divorce already and as a newlywed, he was separated yet again. He was very handsome, young for a doctor, and had many a young nurse drooling over the thought of being his next relationship. I, however, had hardly noticed him until this moment. His eyes were bright blue and his hair was dark and wavy. His complexion was smooth and he was always pristinely dressed, not like a doctor, but more like a preppy. He would merely throw a long, white doctor's coat over his polo shirt and slacks, which barely made him look like he belonged at the hospital, much less like a doctor. The story was that he was older than he appeared and was going through a midlife crisis. His brand new corvette and his secretary with incredibly large breast implants and big hair was a sure sign that there was something to the story. I replied to his blunt comment merely for the sake of conversation, since he had barely spoken to me over the last year.

"Yes, I'm getting a divorce. I hear the same goes for you?"

"Oh yeah, she barely got to use my name and now she wants hers back."

"I'm sorry to hear that. I know how it feels."

"Same here. But you are beautiful and you'll be replacing him soon."

His comment caught me by surprise for several reasons. One, I didn't think of myself as beautiful and especially never thought Dr. Marx would notice if I were, and two, having never spoken to me before, I was surprised that one of his first comments would be so forward. We stood in silence for a couple of moments as we stared at each other before I thanked him for his compliment. His stare was worth a thousand words, and I knew that this was probably the beginning of his pursuit for my attention. I had so many things going on in my head and no idea how I would handle Dr. Marx at that moment. I managed to finish my last half hour of work and headed home.

After my evening unwound, I nervously awaited the kid's return from dinner. I was anxious and felt that something bad was going to happen. I had a tendency towards being superstitious, but nothing ever seemed to come from my feelings, and I hoped that this was just one of those moments where I was all worked up over nothing. About that time, the doorbell rang. It was different now and felt strange at times, having Kyle ring the doorbell to the place he once called home.

I anxiously opened the door and was immediately pushed aside by Katy with her eyes full of tears. She shoved past me and hysterically ran down the hall towards her room, slamming the door. Kyle stood there at the door shaking his head with a smirk on his face. Kaleigh and Levi entered at a much slower pace and I directed them towards their bedrooms so I could speak to Kyle in private.

"What in God's name is going on?"

"It's nothing, really."

"It's obviously something Kyle."

"She's over-reacting just like you Madeline."

"So I gather she has something to over-react to? Possibly something stupid you've said?"

I knew I shouldn't push his buttons, but it seemed that anger was easier to express than the pain and hurt I felt inside. The only way to get it out of my system was with mean and hurtful statements.

"I didn't say anything stupid. I had to tell her the truth."

"What did you tell her Kyle?"

"She wanted to know if I still loved you."

"Oh, GOD, Kyle, please tell me you didn't say that you don't love me anymore. We talked about this and we agreed, and I thought you understood my feelings on this issue."

"I had to tell her the truth, that I didn't love you like a wife. I told her I cared about you as a person, but I didn't love you anymore."

I was so angry. I was hurt and I was so sad for my little Katy. I was so afraid this day would come. I knew that eventually he would probably tell them that he no longer loved me. From the beginning, I begged him not to do so. I felt strongly that if they knew that Daddy could fall out of love with Mommy, then maybe they would think he'd stop loving them too. After all, we had promised each other that we would love each other forever. We had told the kids that we would always be together and that we didn't believe in divorce. With their lives and dreams already shattered, I was sure they would imagine the worst.

I had nothing more to say. Actually, I had a lot more to say, but thanks to Dr. Wesley, I was learning that it was useless to express everything I felt. After 12 years of marriage, I was convinced that Kyle fully understood my expectations, but was hell bent on driving me completely insane. If it weren't for Dr. Wesley, I'd have burnt all of his clothing in the middle of the street like you see in the movies. If I'd had a 2-story house, I'd have thrown all of his belongings out the window to the front yard for the neighbors to see.

There was nothing left for me to say or do except to close the door. My silence would probably do better than any outburst, and I was sure that a tantrum would have only made him feel in control. That was one thing that Dr. Wesley continued to have to remind me of. Kyle had always been a controlling person. But I allowed him to give me permission to wear what he wanted me to wear or to be friends with the people he wanted me to be friends with. But I could no longer allow him the satisfaction of pushing me in the corner until I lost control. So I closed the door. I closed the door with him just standing there.

I spent hours consoling Katy that evening, and although Kaliegh did her best to conceal her pain, I knew that she was affected as well. I put Levi to bed and cuddled with my little broken-hearted girls. The hugging and cuddling was as soothing and comforting to me as it was for them. For every moment that I spent attempting to relieve their pain and discomfort, there was a certain amount of forgetting about my own. I felt a little sad that I would be leaving them over the weekend to go to Tennessee to meet Robert. They didn't know where I was going; they thought it was just to a friend's house. I knew that as mad as I would get at Kyle, he was a good father and I knew they would be in good hands with him. However, I wasn't so sure that I'd be in good hands where I was going, and for a fleeting moment, I felt scared.

The rest of the week was uneventful, until Friday that is. Friday was the day I approached Dr. Wesley about my visit to Tennessee. I felt butterflies in my stomach when I thought about the discussion. I had never lied to Dr. Wesley, and although I was not flat out lying, it would be a stretch of the truth. I would lead him to believe my getaway weekend was as innocent as visiting old friends. He didn't need to know that this was a man that I barely knew and had only met on the internet a few months earlier, and with whom I had only exchanged emails and photographs.

I entered the rehab hospital on Friday morning. I was greeted as usual by the receptionist and exchanged a few words with fellow employees as I walked down the hall to my office. Dr. Wesley was expecting me. I spent every Friday morning in his office. I was nervous; I somehow felt that I had to have his blessing for this trip, but I knew he'd have to be deceived to approve. After a few moments of deep breathing, I picked up the phone and called him. He was ready for me to come over. As I walked the winding halls towards his office, my heart fluttered with anticipation. I hoped that he wouldn't sense my anxiety. I reached his door, and as my hand ever so slightly touched the doorknob, the door opened suddenly.

"Good Morning, Maddie."

"Good Morning, John."

It had only been recently that Dr. Wesley had asked me to call him by his first name. In the beginning it would have been strange, but as our relationship changed from doctor-patient to friendship, it seemed only natural.

"How was your week?"

"It was fine. I had issues with Kyle on Monday. He told the kids that he no longer loved me and they were pretty upset."

"That sounds like the Kyle we know. How is Katy? She must have taken it hard."

"She's fine now. A little talking and a lot of hugging and she seems to have put it behind her."

"So anything exciting planned this weekend?"

"Well, actually, there is. I've been meaning to talk to you about how I need to get away. I think it's time for me to take a break from the divorce and the issues here. I have an opportunity. A friend has bought me a ticket to visit Tennessee for the weekend. I think it would be good for me. My plane leaves tonight and I'll be back on Sunday evening. Short, but sweet."

"Sounds nice. Who is the friend?"

"Their names are Robert & Lara. They are old friends and I think it will be a good break. I want to give you the phone number and address of where I'm staying because I don't want Kyle to know where I'll be. I'm going to give instructions to Kyle that if any emergency arises for the kids, he should contact you if that is ok."

"That's fine Maddie. I think it's a good idea. You need a break."

We spent another half hour talking about feelings, moods, plans for the future, and my job. I was happy that I had his approval and felt good that someone would know my whereabouts, but I felt ashamed that I had not been completely honest. I convinced myself that all I had done was used the words "old friends" instead of "new friend." And of course, using "Robert & Lara" together as if they were a couple instead of father and daughter was also deceiving. I knew that Lara would be with her mother over the weekend and that I would be alone with Robert.

It was less than 12 hours from the time I would board the plane. It would be a difficult day to work. My thoughts were running wild with wonder about what my weekend would be like. The secrecy was almost too much to bear. I didn't share my plans with my friends at work or with Kay; although I knew that Dr. Wesley and Kay were good friends and I was sure he'd mention it to her. We had no patient-doctor confidentiality, since I was not technically his patient. I figured if she brought it up later, I would explain that it was a short getaway and that I had forgotten to mention it. I'd pass it off as a trip to visit friends, no big deal.

When I left Dr. Wesley's office, I made my way to the nurse's station. Brianna was one of the nurse techs in the south wing of the hospital. She was barely 20 years old and was very attractive. She and her sister, Rebecca, had worked at the rehab hospital for about a year. She had an olive complexion, green eyes, and dark brown hair. She was what you'd call a busy body, I guess. She always knew everyone's dating status. She was single and looking and seemed to make it her job to know who was hot and who was not. Today was her day to harass me. I considered Brianna one of my friends, but it was obvious that since my marital status had gone from married to single, that I was now a source of competition for her. Although I had hardly noticed any of the men at work, I was painfully aware that many of them had noticed me. And even if I had not noticed, Brianna would have been sure to bring it to my attention.

When I turned the corner and approached the South Nurses Station, Brianna rose from her chair and practically jumped in my path.

"So Miss Blondie, how's single life treating you?"

Brianna was eight years younger than me and obviously not very experienced with relationships. I was sure she had no idea how painful my separation had been for me. She merely saw my situation as an opportunity for me to engage in free sex with any guy I could get my hands on. She'd often make references to how I could now see what it was like to get laid by someone other than Kyle. In sort of a sick way, she was right. I was curious, and since I was still in a state of believing that true love was no longer a possibility, the potential for unattached sex had often entered my mind. Perhaps my trip this weekend was partially motivated by this curiosity.

"Brianna, get out of my face, I'm not in the mood. And the name is Madeline, not Blondie."

"Oh come on Blondie, I heard about Dr. Marx."

What could she possibly have heard about Dr. Marx? I had a very private, one on one, very brief discussion over spilled papers for probably all of 60 seconds.

"Ok Brianna, now you have my attention, what have you heard?"

"Oh, just that he has the hots for you."

At this point it was obvious that Dr. Marx must have been talking to someone. There had been no conversations regarding him on my part.

"Ok, reveal your sources."

"I can't, I can only say I'm sure of it. So that means you won't be after Blake right?"

"Blake? What are you talking about? Since when have I mentioned Blake?"

Blake was one of the outpatient physical therapists. He was six feet tall with gorgeous blonde hair and beautiful green eyes. Who wouldn't notice him? I noticed Blake when I was still happily married to Kyle. It was impossible not to notice him; he was the epitome of sexy. From his deep, masculine voice, to his tight jeans, when he'd pass by in the halls it was like watching a perfect male specimen; and there were few that would disagree. He once volunteered to give shoulder massages to the employees at the hospital during massage therapy week. Every nurse there, married or single, stood in his line, except me of course. As sexy as he was, I hated flaunting myself in front of men. Even now, he would have to show interest in me before I'd even consider him.

"Brianna, I have never expressed interest in Blake. He's all yours babe. I'm also not after Dr. Marx, so whatever you have heard is false. Get it out of your head."

"Come on Maddie, you know you want Blake. You'd be sick not too."

"Call me sick, I don't want Blake."

Of course, inside, there was an instant vision of my lips touching Blake's, but only for an instant. I grinned as I left the nurse's station, to think for a moment that it might ever happen. For now, I had other things on my mind. I'd be off to meet Robert in a few hours and time was of the essence. I had to finish up my work, hurry home to grab my bags, and take care of a few last minute things before my flight. It was crazy, but it was actually going to happen. It was almost time to meet Robert. My heart seemed to skip a beat as I hurried back to my office.

CHAPTER 5

Meeting A Stranger

When I reached the airport, I called Robert and confirmed my arrival time in Nashville. I was grateful for a smooth check-in process; having only a carry-on will grant that. I love airports; the hustle and bustle of people rushing here and there trying to catch the next plane. If you watch carefully, you'll see lovers parting and families reuniting. It's like a game for me, creating stories in my head about the people I see. Perhaps there was a couple meeting in person for the first time after an encounter on the internet. If not, there would be shortly.

My trip was only four hours, including my stop in Houston. It was hard to believe that in just four hours, I would be meeting a man who was a perfect stranger only a few months ago. It didn't feel like something I would ever do. But then again, I had been through so much that I was a different person now. My entire life had been turned upside down. This was only a beginning step in the many changes that I would experience. As I sat and waited for the plane to board, I thought about Robert. Somehow I knew that this would be a temporary relationship. I knew that even though he'd been very nice to me and he seemed like a great person, there was something inside that kept telling me he was only a diversion and would not be a constant in my life.

I heard the announcement to board the plane, grabbed my

bags, and headed to the gate. It felt like an unusually long walk to the plane. Thoughts passed through my mind, thoughts of my kids, Kyle, my mother. I felt a little awkward, like I shouldn't be there. I found my seat and was relieved to find that I was sitting next to an attractive female. It was better than sitting next to a balding, overweight, middle-aged man the entire trip. I threw my large carry-on bag in the bin above the seat, squeezed past the aisle seat and the woman in the middle, and found my seat by the window. I loved the window seat, partly because I could gaze out the window to the world below, but mostly because I had control of the shade if the sun should bother me. I stowed my purse under the seat in front of me. As the plane took off, it occurred to me that there was no turning back. I would be meeting Robert in a few hours.

My flight to Tennessee was a perfect opportunity for me to reflect on my life. If nothing else, it was peaceful and calming to be flying in the opposite direction of my troubles. My stop in Houston was uneventful and it seemed like only a short time before we were descending towards Nashville. The passengers all began to rustle for belongings and you could almost feel the anticipation of the arrival. The woman next to me decided to make conversation, and although I'm the talkative type, there was a part of me that hoped she wouldn't ask me where I was going. I was not entirely comfortable with my decision to meet Robert in the first place, and wasn't sure if I should reveal my plan to a stranger. But then, there was a little fear factor involved. I thought that maybe if I told this person what I was doing, and I felt uncomfortable when I met Robert, that she could be my safety net. There I was planning my escape in case of disaster and to make matters worse, my escape was yet another complete stranger. I decided that my plan was silly, but as she asked me if I was visiting Nashville or if I lived there, I decided that sharing might be just what I needed at the moment, so I went for it.

"I'm meeting someone in Nashville that I met on the internet."

MEETING A STRANGER

"No way!"

"Yes, he asked me to meet him and I accepted."

"Do you know what he looks like? Aren't you scared? Wow, I could never do that."

"We've been exchanging emails and he sent me his picture. I've spoken to him on the phone and I've talked to his daughter. I think he's a nice person. I feel safe."

Inside, I wasn't completely convinced that I was safe, but if felt good to hear myself say it. Part of me felt just as crazy as I knew this woman thought I was. I was wearing a very cute, short dress, and had described the dress to Robert so he could easily identify me. It was cold outside, but I wanted to make a good impression. He agreed to have a red rose in his hand and be waiting by the gate. I had seen his picture, but it was small and I wasn't sure I'd recognize him. You hear about people sending old, outdated pictures over the internet and then they turn out to be 20 years older and 50 pounds heavier. I'm sure he was wondering the same thing, since I had sent him the picture I had taken for Kyle for our anniversary a few months prior to our separation; the same picture that caused so much controversy shortly before the end of our relationship.

It was a couple months prior to our 12th wedding anniversary and I wasn't sure what type of a gift to give Kyle. He had become obsessed with my body since I began working out at a nearby gym that friends of ours had opened. My friend, Amy, and I had been running five miles per day, and I was in the best shape I had ever been. I thought it was a great idea to have my portrait made as a gift for Kyle. I wanted something different, something more than just a studio posed portrait. My sister had friends that were photographers and I made arrangements to travel to Monahans, Texas to have my photo taken at the sand hills. Although I knew the photographers, I also knew that Kyle would not approve of two men being alone with me and taking my photo. They were brothers, one of which was single and the other going through a divorce. Monahans was a good hour drive and we'd need to take my van to transport the equipment. This brought Courtney into the picture. Since our husbands were firefighters and both on the same shift, I could take her with me sort of as a chaperone. If need be, she could testify that it was all in innocence since Kyle was the jealous type.

I decided on a bikini for the portrait to show my figure and have something for Kyle to be proud of. Most of the firefighters had pictures of their girlfriends and wives in their locker. Kyle never had one and this was my opportunity to change that. Courtney and I had the entire day planned. I would wait until Kyle left for the fire station and then I'd call Courtney, who would meet me at the photography studio, and we'd be off for a day in the sand. My mother kept the kids that day and everything went just as planned. I had my van vacuumed to remove all of the sand and was careful to fill my tank up with gas so Kyle wouldn't notice anything.

I received the pictures a week and a half before our anniversary. They were stunning. It was hard to believe they were photos of me. I had the largest print framed and carefully wrapped it and hid it under the bed. Courtney was as excited about the reveal as I was. The problem began when Courtney told her husband Mark about the photo shoot. I didn't blame her, he was her husband and they didn't keep secrets. The bad part was that Mark didn't seem to keep secrets either. I was sure the leak came from him telling another firefighter about the pictures. Kyle had returned from work only days before our anniversary and was noticeably upset. He approached me in our bedroom after the kids had gone to bed.

"What is with the pictures?"

"What pictures?"

"There is talk all over the fire station about, you and some calendar."

"What are you talking about?"

"I don't know exactly what I'm talking about but I think you do."

MEETING A STRANGER

  I did my best to pass the subject off as some silly gossip that had no ring of truth to it, but Kyle could see right through me. I had never been a good liar, and although this lie was a white lie to cover up a fun surprise, it was none-the-less a lie. After a little more pressure, I finally broke down and cried. I explained the whole story and tried to reassure Kyle, but he insisted on seeing the picture now, not on our anniversary. I pulled the picture out from under the bed and he proceeded to tear off the packaging. His reaction was not what I expected. He was very upset that two male photographers had taken the pictures. Instead of feeling like his beautiful wife who gave him a gift from the heart, I felt like a deceitful slut that should be ashamed of what I had done. Our anniversary was not so great that year, and in hindsight, it makes perfect sense. Kyle never trusted me because he didn't trust himself. It's like the saying always goes, the guilty dog barks first. He was sure that if he was having desires to cheat that his wife must be also. The picture hung in our bedroom, and when company came, it was placed in the closet out of sight as if it were something to be ashamed of.

  In the picture I sent to Robert, I was wearing a floral bikini top and very short denim shorts, with the button and zipper undone just enough to reveal my bikini bottoms underneath. It was probably a little too sexy of a picture to share with someone prior to meeting for the first time, but I was proud of it and it was the most recent picture I had. I took most of the pictures of our family, which meant that I was almost never in them.

  I realized that meeting Robert would be even more awkward, since the woman sitting next to me was interested in our meeting and would be observing if she could. I was not only concerned with what I'd think of him but what she'd think of him as well. But then again, I would probably never see this woman again, so I decided it was not worth worrying about.

  The fasten seatbelt light came on as we prepared for landing. My heart raced as I envisioned the entire meeting in my mind. I had a multitude of emotions in my body. It was a thrill if nothing else. I would have to compare that moment with the feeling you get on a roller-coaster ride with abrupt twists, breathtaking bumps, and a sudden 50-foot drop. Your stomach sinks, your heart practically stops, and although you are scared stiff, you are filled with excitement. The tires of the plane screeched as they met the runway. My seatbelt tightened and I felt nauseous. I wasn't sure if it was the landing causing the sensation or the anticipation of the meeting.

As the other passengers rushed to get off the plane, I took my time. I wasn't trying to make Robert think I didn't come; I was merely trying to gather the courage to walk off the plane. The experience was definitely outside my comfort zone, but being the adventurous type I eventually mustered up the strength to get off the plane. Pretty much every person had left the plane and I was still gathering my bags. I slowly headed down the ramp towards the airport. As I entered the concourse, I heard voices, and laughter, of children, men, and women. I wasn't sure which direction to go, and the many voices and faces of people I'd never seen before were distracting me. This was the first time I'd arrived at an airport without a familiar face to greet me.

Up ahead to my left, I saw a man that resembled the picture I received via email. He was clean cut, dressed in suit pants and a dress shirt, and was holding a red rose. As I headed towards him, I could tell he recognized me. It was a very strange moment, and as I approached him, I realized that he was much shorter than I had imagined. I figured that a picture of him kneeling by a rock wouldn't show his true height. His face, although similar to the picture, was different. In the picture, he was facing the front so his profile was not revealed. Although he was not ugly by any means, he was definitely not what I had imagined. I'd almost reached where he stood and I realized that I wasn't exactly sure how to greet him on our first meeting. Should I hug him, shake his hand, or kiss his cheek? Although I must have gone over this moment a thousand times in my mind, I felt so unprepared.

MEETING A STRANGER

As I reached him, there was a formal verification that I had the right guy and vice versa, and I guess hugging was the most natural thing to do. A hug is somewhat more personal than a handshake, but less intimate than a kiss. Over his shoulder, I could see the woman I sat next to on the plane staring my direction with a huge smile on her face. At this point, she could only see Robert's back, and I could tell she was stretching to get a better view.

Robert handed me the rose and I thanked him. I wasn't sure if he could sense my discomfort or not. He was smiling and seemed almost giddy with excitement, like something he had purchased by mail order had finally arrived. The truth is, that is just about what happened; you might call it email-order. Of course, it would be expected for me to be a bit more nervous due to the fact that I was completely out of familiar surroundings. We exchanged overall looks at each other for a moment, and then Robert broke the silence.

"You look exactly like your picture."

I felt obligated to say the same of him, but he actually looked quite different. I realized at that moment that although a picture is worth a thousand words, a thousand written words might not be enough to describe a person. There is so much that you don't know until you meet someone in the physical form. Their scent, the way their mouth moves when words are spoken, their entire demeanor, all of it is completely lost with communication through email. Although we had exchanged a lot of information and I knew a lot about Robert, I still felt as though I was meeting a stranger.

We headed towards the parking garage. The walk was awkward. Robert reached out to hold my hand, but it didn't feel natural. It was almost like being a teenager in school again. I kept looking around as if I were searching for a familiar face. There were only strange people, strange sights, and strange surroundings. Even the woman that I sat by on the plane was nowhere to be seen; so much for my plan of escape. This was it. I was in Nashville, Tennessee. I was here for the weekend with Robert.

CHAPTER 6

Music City

It was immediately apparent that Robert was not short on money when we approached his expensive car. My thoughts drifted back to Dr. Marx at the hospital, and the stories of his fancy cars and the connection to his supposed mid-life crisis. Was this a similar situation? It seemed all of the divorced women I knew drove mini-vans and the divorced men drove sport cars. Perhaps the sports car was a way of luring attractive, younger women to an older man. I didn't know Robert's actual age, but he was about 10 to 12 years older than me, somewhere close to 40. His age didn't bother me; I saw it as a sign of maturity and stability.

He leaned over and opened the passenger door for me. I stepped inside and he tossed my bag in the trunk. It was already past midnight, but I wasn't tired, probably due to the adrenaline surge from the anticipation of our meeting. I never slept much anyway. I'd always been somewhat of an insomniac.

"Are you hungry?"

"Actually, I'm starving. Somehow airline pretzels just don't cut it for dinner."

"I know a place we can get some food. They are open till 2 a.m."

"Great!"

◄ BEYOND THE PRESENT

"Do you want to eat at the bar or would you prefer to take it to my house?"

I was eager to get to his house. I wanted to get my bearings. I needed to feel comfortable with my surroundings and prepare for the weekend.

"Let's get take out."

Robert picked up his mobile phone and dialed a number. When he started talking, he sounded like he was talking to an old friend instead of a restaurant or bar. He took the initiative to order for me. I thought that was a little brave as he didn't really know me and couldn't be sure of what I'd want to eat. But I was starving and happy with just about anything.

It was a short drive to the establishment where he ordered our food. I wasn't sure what kind of place it would be, but it turned out to be sort of club like. As we entered the front door, there was little room for standing. The place was packed. To my surprise, several people greeted Robert by name and immediately engaged in small talk with him. He held my hand and sort of dragged me through the crowd towards the bar. People seemed to know Robert and certainly took notice of me. Once again, the bartender knew Robert by name.

"Hey, Robert. Good to see you, your food is on the way out."

With over 500,000 people in Nashville, it seemed strange to me that people here would know Robert by name. I knew he was not in the restaurant business and decided this must be a place he frequently visited. From our letters and chat conversations, I had taken him for a very lonely person, yet this evening it seemed that friends surrounded him.

We rushed out as quickly as we entered. As we headed towards his house, the beauty of the glistening snow on the ground enthralled me. There was little snow in the West Texas city I had come from, only cold winds that would chill you to your bones. The storms that Tennessee had received this year were a burden to the residents, but magical to tourists like myself. The drive to his house was mostly silent. I'm not sure if I was too nervous to speak or if we just didn't have words to share. I knew almost instantly when meeting Robert at the airport that there was no chemistry between us. This fact would have been helpful upon making my decision to visit or not to visit, but that was behind me now and I needed to make the best of this situation. Realistically, I didn't expect Robert to be the man of my dreams. The man of my dreams was Kyle, and we were no longer together. This trip would hopefully give me a much-needed break from reality. Robert didn't strike me as a sex-driven maniac, and I felt relatively safe as we continued the drive.

I was impressed with his house from the minute we approached the driveway. The eaves were covered with snow and the details in the gables reminded me of a gingerbread house from a children's book. Being an older home, there was no garage, and my sexy dress was much to flimsy for the weather. The jacket I brought was not heavy enough to keep me warm. Robert grabbed my bag as I carried the take-out food, and we hurried up the steps to the front door. When we entered, the snow from our shoes melted onto the warm wool rug beneath our feet. The floors were covered in a rich, dark-stained, hardwood. The furnishings in his entry and living area were inviting. Robert had prepared a bottle of wine in an ice bucket on the large, wooden coffee table in front of the fireplace, along with two long-stem wine glasses. A large rug lay in front of the fireplace. Robert immediately took my jacket and hung it on hook in the entry area. He took the bag of food from me, placed it on the coffee table in his living area, and began preparing a fire.

"Make yourself comfortable."

I took my shoes off and sat on his oversized sofa. I looked around the room and it seemed as though his home had been professionally decorated. I couldn't imagine a single man having done all of this alone.

The room was filled with rich woods. The kitchen, which was

in plain view from the living area, had been updated with more modern amenities. His home was cozy, and I was immediately comforted by my surroundings. It was apparent that Robert was the romantic type. His sofa table was covered with candles and pictures of his daughter. On the far right side of the table was my picture. He had placed it carefully into a rich, cherry wood frame. Seeing my picture there felt as if I belonged in his home. We sat on the sofa and ate our food in front of the fire.

After we were finished dining, Robert pulled out a photo album. He began to show me pictures of his former wife and his daughter Lara. He browsed through the last 10 years of his life and connected stories with many pictures. I listened intently for the first few pages and then my mind began to wander. I thought about how one day I would be sitting on a sofa with another man sharing my life stories about Kyle and our three children through the pages of a photo album. It seemed so sad, and I suddenly lost interest in Robert's stories. He must have noticed that I was distracted because he asked me if everything was ok.

"I'm not really in the mood to look at family photos right now. My family has only recently been broken and I'd rather think of other things."

"I'm sorry Maddie, I guess that was thoughtless on my part."

"No, Robert, it's perfectly normal that you would share your photos with me. It's me who is not perfectly normal right now."

I was starting to feel cold and I moved down to the floor next to the fireplace. Robert tossed me a pillow from the sofa and I lay down on the floor next to the crackling fire. The heat from the fire seemed to bathe me in warmth, and the light from the flame flickered across the wooden floor in the dimly lit room.

"Do you mind if I join you?"

I didn't answer. I wasn't sure what to say. I was lonely, and although the fire warmed my body, my heart felt cold. Robert crawled off the sofa to the floor behind me. He scooted up against my body and I felt his arm come over the front of my waist. The rug was soft, and had there been chemistry between us, I'm sure this would have been a very romantic encounter. With the absence of physical desire, this potentially romantic moment was now just a sad reminder of what could have been with Kyle.

"What are you thinking?"

"I'm wondering how many men I will lie next to in front of a fire before I find love again."

"Don't think so deep Maddie, just enjoy the moment."

This remark was all too familiar. Kyle had often told me that I think too much. He was more of a live for the moment person and I was the planner. Maybe this was a male/female difference, but it reminded me so much of Kyle. Ironically, the very reason I accepted Robert's invitation was to stop thinking about Kyle, and as I lay in front of his fireplace, memories of Kyle flooded my mind. It was late and Robert had big plans to show me Nashville on Saturday. I wondered what the sleeping arrangements would be and what Robert expected of me. As a true gentleman, he offered me his daughter Lara's room, which I gladly accepted. Lara now lived with her mother and only visited every other weekend, so her room was available.

As I retired to his daughter's room for the night, I pulled a slinky satin nightgown out of my bag and slipped out of my dress. I pulled the nightgown over my head and the satin draped over my body. It was cold next to my skin, and in the mirror across the room, I could see the curves of my breasts and the lines around my nipples through the fabric. It was a sexy nightgown, as were most of the clothing items I had brought on this trip. It was very cold in Nashville, and my wardrobe hardly fit the weather. Fortunately, I'd packed a warm, fuzzy sweater for our outing on Saturday, when Robert planned to show me the town.

I folded back the covers on Lara's full size bed and sat down on the cold sheets. I took a look around the room and realized how lonely I was. I lay in the bed alone and closed my eyes, but I couldn't sleep. After about 15 minutes, I sat up again. I swung my feet to the cold wood floor and stared towards the door. I wondered what it would feel like to lie in bed with a man beside me again. Sometimes, it seemed like yesterday that I had Kyle lying next to me in bed, and other times it felt like ages had passed. It wasn't sex that I needed or craved at that moment, it was companionship. I wished that I could remember the last time I slept in bed with Kyle or the last time we made love. I often thought about how, if I had known that it would be the last time, that I would have taken mental notes so as never to forget the feel of his last touch or the caress of his lips against my breast.

I acted on impulse as I headed towards the door, and my heart beat rapidly as it opened. Lara's bedroom was a safe haven and meant that I would make no mistakes, at least for the rest of the night. Once I walked through the door, what followed was unknown. The door squeaked when I opened it. Robert had shown me where the bathroom was, and I was sure if he heard me he'd expect that was where I was going. I proceeded down the hall towards the bathroom and stopped when I reached Robert's bedroom door. I turned to face his room and then gently knocked on his door. I heard him say, "Come In." His voice was gentle and soft. As I opened the door, I saw Robert lying in his bed across the room. His blankets were pulled up to his waist and he lay there with no shirt on. He was a slight built man with dark hair, and he had a gentle look about his face.

"Can I sleep in here? I'm lonely."

"Of course, Maddie. There is plenty of room here."

He slid over to make room for me, although his bed was already large enough for both of us. I slid under the covers and pulled myself close to his body. He was warm, as was his bed, and he gently placed his arm around my back as I lay my head on his shoulder. I placed my hand on his chest and could feel his heart racing. He seemed so calm and collected, yet his heart raced as though he'd been running a marathon. I instantly felt relaxed and safe with him, and without a word exchanged between us, I drifted off to sleep.

It was Saturday morning and when I woke, I found myself in Robert's bed alone. I could hear him stirring in the kitchen and I could smell food. I was surprised that Robert hadn't made any advances and that I was brave enough to crawl in bed next to him knowing that he might.

I could feel the crispness in the air. It was a cold morning and I was snuggled warm under the covers, but the fresh aroma of breakfast and the scent of burning firewood seemed to lure me out of bed. As I pulled myself up to a sitting position, I found a fresh, white robe at the foot of the bed. It was neatly folded and had a red rose bud lying atop with a hand scribbled note, "Good Morning Sunshine."

I slipped my arms in the robe, tied the front and stepped barefoot onto the rug beneath the bed. I wandered through the hall past the living area and the brightly burning fire to the large kitchen. Robert was dressed and busily scurrying around the kitchen, preparing what appeared to be a gourmet breakfast. He caught a glimpse of me over his shoulder and turned towards me with a smile on his face.

"It's a beautiful day! I'm giving a beautiful woman a tour of the Music City. What could be better?"

Robert had a way with words. He was a true romantic and seemed to flatter me constantly. I couldn't figure him out. He seemed so sweet and gentlemanly, but surely he expected something from me. After all, he purchased my round trip ticket and went out of his way to make plans to wine and dine me for the entire weekend. Yet, he seemed to have no ulterior motives. I remember him stating in one of his emails how he remembered the pain right after his divorce and he hated to see me going through it. He spoke of wishing he'd had someone to talk to and to distract him from his misery during that time. Maybe he was a saint and truly was interested in being a good person and being there for me in my time of need. On the other hand, I couldn't imagine any man passing up a perfect opportunity to have sex, no strings attached, with an attractive, single woman who was at his house the entire weekend. In fact, many men, married and single alike, had already attempted to make their move back at home, some of them friends of Kyle's. It was almost eerie the way Robert seemed to give me my space. There was a little piece of me that for a second wondered if he was actually a psycho waiting for the right time to attack.

After breakfast, we spent all of Saturday morning and afternoon touring Nashville's many attractions. Robert shared my passion for art and we toured museums and galleries. We visited posh boutiques and small, fashionable shops. We ate lunch at a downtown bar & grille and walked the streets of Nashville, with me bundled in the new coat I purchased in order to keep from freezing in the snow. I mentioned my favorite perfume to Robert and he generously purchased a large bottle for me at a local perfume shop.

It was nearing Saturday evening and even after the wonderful day that Robert had so carefully planned, I was still thinking only of Kyle. I was wishing that our life together had not ended so abruptly. I spent almost every romantic moment that day wishing that I was with Kyle instead of Robert. And although Robert had great plans for dinner, all I wanted to do was drown in my sorrow.

Robert had planned an exquisite evening at a restaurant with a casually elegant, upscale atmosphere. He knew how much I loved steak and lobster and planned everything carefully. I dressed the part, wearing my most elegant yet sexy dress. As we prepared for our evening, I poured my first glass of wine. This was probably my first mistake of the weekend. I have a very low tolerance for alcohol and Kyle had often referred to me as a cheap date. On occasion, I had passed out from only a few glasses of wine; of course, unfortunately, I never passed out before making a total fool of myself.

However, there was one particular time that my low tolerance of wine proved useful to me. It was only a few months before Kyle had left me that I had suspected that he had been entertaining himself through phone sex. Our phone bill had skyrocketed and Kyle made no attempt to hide the bills. When I approached him, he swore that he never made the calls. Since we had no teenage boys in the house and I was certain I was not sharing my body with split personalities, the only possible culprit was Kyle.

One particular evening, I downed a glass of wine after putting the kids to bed and lured Kyle in the bedroom, holding a half empty wine bottle in my hand. As soon as I got him all worked up and turned on, I pretended to crash from the effects of the wine. At this point, I wasn't sure if he'd give up and go to sleep or proceed to have his way with me. To my surprise, as I lay naked in the bed, I heard Kyle pick up the phone receiver. I could hear the tones of the phone pad and within minutes I could hear Kyle's voice softly speaking into the phone as he caressed my naked body. It was evident through his words and his tone of voice that he was speaking to a woman on the other end of the phone and describing what he was doing to me. He proceeded to have sex with me as I lay there pretending to be unconscious. He remained on the phone the entire time. It was quick, and obviously the excitement of the phone call did the trick for him. I never confessed to him that I had faked passing out that night, and instead called the phone company and blamed the calls on a house guest and had them block 900 calls from our number.

As Robert and I prepared for dinner and I sipped my wine, my sensitivity to the concoction escaped me. We grabbed our coats and headed out the door. Robert was a perfect gentleman. He opened every door and pulled out my chair at dinner. By the time I had the menu in front of me, my nose had become numb from the effects of the wine I drank before leaving his house. That was my trademark, my numb nose. It was as if the alcohol was warning me that I should stop by numbing my nose. It seemed extremely silly to me and I made a big deal out of how I could no longer feel my nose. We laughed about it and ordered the lobster and steak.

The price of my meal was outrageous, but by now I had become accustomed to Robert's pampering. I ordered another glass of wine and it seemed to go down even faster and smoother than the first. Of course Robert was not aware of my "cheap date syndrome" and he ordered a third glass before my second was finished. By the time my food arrived, I had no more appetite. I was giggling uncontrollably and Robert seemed amused.

I needed to make my way to the ladies room and was aware that I was seriously impaired at this point. Robert pointed out the direction to the restroom just beyond the bar. I managed to pull myself to my feet and staggered towards the bar through the closely placed tables. It was Saturday night and the restaurant was packed. Near the bar, there was a group of men standing around, laughing, and engaging in conversation. They saw me coming and I was an obvious, easy target. As I passed through them to make my way to the restroom they closed in on me and I felt hands groping beneath the skirt of my already short dress. As I managed to free myself from their grasps, I stumbled forward, only to be caught by the same men who then managed to fondle my breasts while helping me up. In my intoxicated state, it never bothered me a bit and I just continued to make my way to the restroom. After my third glass of wine, Robert had decided to cut our date short, considering that I was probably not going to last much longer. He boxed up my lobster dinner and managed to get me into the car.

When we arrived back at Robert's house, I could barely stand on my own two feet. Everything was still so funny and I gleefully jumped out of the car without my jacket. The temperature was below freezing outside, but it didn't seem to affect me. I was warm inside from the alcohol, and as Robert threw my coat around my shoulders, he scooped me up in his arms. Although he was not much larger than me, he was much stronger, and my drunken weight didn't seem to affect his ability to carry me up the stairs to his entry.

He laid me on his couch and I started to giggle as I reached for his shoulders and pulled him onto me. I was plastered, and I knew that under the influence I would lose all of my inhibitions. Robert had been such a gentleman and now I was pulling him on top of me and the alcohol was taking control. No matter how much he may have wanted to resist, there was probably not a man alive who would not give in to my insatiable desire at that moment.

We made out on the couch and he slipped my pantyhose off beneath my dress. His hand caressed my inner thigh and he proceeded to have his way with me. I must have been in and out of consciousness, or perhaps the alcohol caused memory loss, because although I'm sure we had sex, I can hardly recall the act itself. What seemed like only moments later, but in actuality was over an hour, I found myself in his bathtub with running water at my feet and bubbles up to my face. Robert sat on a nearby bench and I saw my clothes piled at the foot of the tub. He stared at me with gentle eyes. I was surprised that I didn't remember getting undressed and getting in the tub. In the background I could hear music. He was playing my favorite songs. I was amazed at what a wonderful person I had stumbled upon. It was too bad that I had no romantic feelings towards him. I wasn't sure why they didn't exist, but I was sure that there were no sparks. He had been more like a friend to me.

I sat up in the tub and reached for the water. I turned it to the off position and sat in the bubbles silently. The silence was short lived as I began to spill my guts.

"I'm sorry you brought me here for this. I'm sorry I ruined our date. You spent so much money on me and I didn't even eat it. I'm really sorry, you must be sick of me and ready for me to leave."

"Maddie, don't be so hard on yourself. You needed this break, and you needed to be carefree for once in your life. Besides, lobster is great for breakfast."

"Why are you being so nice to me? Why do you care?"

"I told you Maddie, I've been there, done that."

I stood up in the tub. There was no reason to be shy because he had already seen it all. The suds trickled over my breasts and ran down my stomach.

"You are beautiful." He said.

I reached for a towel and wrapped my naked body in it. I stepped out of the tub onto the soft, thick rug. I stepped close to the bench where Robert sat, and as I leaned forward, I kissed the top of his head and whispered a soft thank you. I had no interest in a continuing a physical relationship with him. Whatever happened that night was an affect of the alcohol.

My departure was scheduled for early Sunday afternoon. Although my visit was short, it was better that way. Had I any interest in continuing a relationship with him, I could always plan a much longer trip to spend time with him in the future.

On Sunday, at the airport before departing, I gave Robert a very long, sultry goodbye kiss. I knew this kiss would be goodbye and I wanted to give him something to remember me by, although I had probably already done that in the previous two evenings. He promised that he would keep in touch and that he would never forget me. I knew that this would be my one and only trip to Nashville to visit Robert, but I didn't share that information. I figured that some things are better left unsaid. As I turned to board the plane, I thought of my children and the life that awaited me back home. There was no escaping reality. This was only a brief interlude. My life would continue and I had to face the real music that awaited me at home, with Music City behind me.

CHAPTER 7

Confrontation

It was back to life as usual upon my return. Late February was just as cold as January had been and I longed for spring. I had decided to sell my house. I wasn't comfortable anymore in the town where Kyle and I had married so many years before. There were mutual friends that had taken sides, and the few who had taken my side, I lost when I abandoned my religion.

Then there was my business selling my artwork to firefighters in the form of t-shirts. I would draw intricate, detailed drawings of the fire trucks and transfer the images onto garments, which were acceptable for them to wear around the fire station. I knew so many of them, yet firefighters form an unusual bond and I knew that no matter how hard I tried to be accepted, I'd never again be selling shirts to them. There were the few firefighters that continued to pursue a relationship with me, which did not interest me at all. I felt it was time to move on and build new relationships in a new place.

Kyle and I had often discussed moving to California. His parents lived near San Francisco and we felt that it would be good for the kids to be exposed to both sets of grandparents. Kyle had talked about still wanting to move there and we had discussed that if I were to sell the house and move that he would follow to be close to the kids and his parents. So I put the house on the market.

BEYOND THE PRESENT

We had purchased the home when I found out I was pregnant with Levi, and after remodeling it, I felt sure that I would make enough to cover my move to California.

I sat at my computer, feeling a sense of guilt about my weekend with Robert. I felt I had led him to believe that there could be a relationship between us, when deep down, I was aware the entire time that it wasn't possible this soon after the breakup. Not only was I not ready for a relationship, I had no interest in moving to Nashville, and now that we had met, I knew that he was not my type. Kyle seemed to be on to something and was curious about my secrecy about where I had gone for the weekend. I should have guessed that he would figure it out, as he was a master of deceit. I have never been good at lying, so when he questioned me, it was easier to avoid the subject than to make up a story.

It was Saturday and it was time to bring the kids to Kyle's apartment for a visit. He had requested in advance that I stay for a few minutes to talk. I wasn't sure what the subject would be, but a part of me knew he was going to drill me on where I had been during the previous weekend. Kyle had confessed his sins, and it was as though he was consumed with forcing me to find the error of my ways and confess mine as well.

I gathered the kid's weekend clothes, toothbrushes, hair bows, and a few toys and packed them in the car and headed to Kyle's. They were giddy and excited about Daddy's new apartment. He had converted a front closet into a toy room for them, and it seemed that with each visit it was packed with new things to entertain them. Each weekend visit with Daddy was filled with treats; ice cream, movies, toys, and the like, which made being home with Mommy seem like prison. At Daddy's, there was constant play and it was an escape from reality. On the contrary, Mommy's was where homework, chores, and mundane routines existed. Daddy was like the every-other weekend babysitter.

When we arrived, Kyle had a few new toys on the patio of his apartment. The weather had warmed a bit and the kids were

CONFRONTATION

quickly escorted out of ears reach so Kyle could begin our conversation. In the beginning, I was surprised by a sense that he had a true desire to have a conversation and not a fight. But little did I know that he was just good at disguise. Perhaps I wanted so desperately to have some civil type of relationship or maybe I was just good at being fooled. He proceeded to tell me how we had become two different people and that we were too young to marry in the first place. Although his statement didn't change the hurt that he had caused me, I couldn't disagree with his reasoning. He explained how, via the internet, he had finally met someone that he could talk to who could understand him and how it made him realize how different we were.

I guess he knew me pretty well because just listening to him created an overwhelming desire inside me to reveal my secrets. It wasn't that I needed to share, but inside I was hurting and was under some pretense that if I were to reveal my secret relationship with Robert that Kyle would also experience some sort of pain. Unbeknownst to me, this was merely a trap. I opened my mouth and out came my secret.

"I happened to meet someone on the internet as well. It's nice to finally talk to someone who doesn't say that I think too much."

That was all he needed. It was fuel for the fire. Instantly, I knew that he had not been confiding in me. This was his way of finding out what had been going on. Kyle was obviously suffering from what I call the "Don't want you but don't want anyone else to have you syndrome." Lucky for me, before I had a chance to reveal that I had gone to Tennessee to meet this someone, Kyle went into a verbal frenzy. He was very upset and his voice became elevated. I knew I couldn't let him find out that I had gone to see Robert, because whether he wanted full custody of the kids or not, I knew he would use it against me to prove me unfit in some way. Even if I was wrong and he wouldn't use it in court, I couldn't take any chances.

"I knew it, I knew it. I knew you had been seeing someone. You've been seeing someone all along haven't you?"

He knew that I had not been unfaithful during our marriage. It was as though he needed to make himself believe that I was reprehensible in order to relieve his own guilt. I let him ramble and turned my attention towards the kids. I could see that Kyle was angry and in some ways it made me feel less trapped and more successful in evening out the score. I decided to let him believe whatever he wished. It was at this time that I realized that I could never confide in Kyle again and that our relationship had definitely changed forever. It was as if this was a turning point in my mind. Instead of letting the pain consume me, I realized that it was time to move forward. This whole meeting was just another way for Kyle to attempt to control me. I had to take control of my life. Part of taking control would mean excluding Kyle from any information about my personal life. I would have to limit my connection with him strictly to the children. They were, after all, all we had in common at this point. While Kyle was still talking, I turned towards the patio. My only escape was to have the kids present so he would back off.

"Katy, Kaleigh, Levi, I have to go now, give Mommy a hug."

This infuriated Kyle. As the kids ran towards me he stopped talking, but the look in his eyes was enough to know that this wasn't the end of the conversation. I quickly gave the kids a hug and briefly confirmed the arrangements for Kyle to drop them off Sunday night. It wouldn't be long before our divorce was final and I would have to continue to be quiet about anything and everything I did. I knew already that Kyle could not be trusted and if it was true that he no longer loved me, there would be nothing to stop him from attempting to ruin my life even further.

I turned and left Kyle's apartment and headed towards the parking lot. I had approximately 32 more hours of lonely weekend left before the kids returned home. When we first separated, I used to look forward to the weekends that the kids were with Kyle. I used those weekends to lie in bed and feel sorry for myself. It seemed like a good use of time. But now, I was beginning to be-

CONFRONTATION

come bored of loneliness. I felt the need to have something to do, or someone to take care of. With no friends to turn to and no one to pick up after, my weekends were slow and painful. The only place I had to turn was the internet. It was there that I had built another life. A life without cares, where I could mold the Madeline that I had become into someone that I longed to be.

I spent the entire Saturday and all of Saturday night chatting and meeting new people. Most of the people I had met were interesting and entertaining to say the least. A lesbian woman sharing her feelings on why women had no use for men, a young man bored and looking for attractive females to chat with, and an elderly gentlemen with poetry to share. It was merely a way to pass the time.

But in the midst of the idle chat and outrageous entertainment, there was a man who caught my attention. His name was Greg, and he was open and honest about his purpose for being there. He was divorced after 12 years of marriage, exactly like me, and he was a father of two young girls. He was different than most of the others. He insisted that he was only there for conversation, similar to me. He often invited his best friend to join our chat sessions. His friend lived pretty far from him and this was also an opportunity for them to keep in touch.

His friend, Jason, was a bit crude and obviously bored with his marriage and only interested in meeting girls that excited him. Greg and I would discuss children, the difference between men and women, and the weather, but when he'd invite Jason, the conversation would take a turn and we'd be debating the nature of sex, the ability or inability for a man to be faithful, and the intrigue of the ménage trois. Jason was less interested in the person he was chatting with and more interested in talking about sex. I often wondered if he even cared if I really was a woman or not. Greg was always eloquent and would take my side in heated debates with Jason. A few times, Jason would sign off irritated and accuse Greg of being a traitor.

BEYOND THE PRESENT

I continued my conversations with Greg over the next month. We chatted nightly and on the weekends that Kyle had the kids; I'd stay up all night chatting with him. We even exchanged addresses so that we could send cards and hand written letters. He was a public speaker and a communications expert, and his philosophies intrigued me. He often talked about the philosophy of objectivism and even sent me a book by Ayn Rand. I hardly skimmed the book but hearing what he had to say was extremely interesting. I couldn't help but compare him to Kyle. Kyle's education was limited to his training as a paramedic and he had no interest in any philosophical conversation. In fact, Kyle and I had little in common when it came to the art of conversation. He felt that I talked too much and would often belittle me when I would introduce a controversial subject merely for the sake of conversation.

Greg was a lot like Robert when it came to his conversational style and his level of intelligence. It seemed that I was drawn more towards intellect than the brute strength that had once been the object of my affection. Perhaps it was the desire to find something different than what I had shared with Kyle for 12 years. Perhaps I longed for someone to give me something opposite so that my memories of Kyle would fade and I could find some sense of happiness without every conversation reminding me of something I once had. The internet had become a sense of comfort for me. A place where I had friends; friends who didn't know everything that had happened in my life and didn't judge me based on the circumstances I faced or the decisions I made. They were real people with real problems who were all seeking a "different" world to escape from the mundane lives they led. We were all people with common interests and it satisfied me for the time being. But I was aware that it would only be a matter of time before the non-physical relationships I had built in this semi-real place would be unable to fill my emptiness.

CHAPTER 8

Lonely

It was Monday morning, and I had dropped the girls off at school and left Levi with my mother. I was early today, which was great because today I was eager to get to work. The weekends had become boring and by Sunday night I longed for the adult companionship that I received from fellow employees. I found the idle gossip that spread through the nurse's station like an epidemic intriguing. I didn't want to start the gossip or continue it, but just listening to the stories of other people helped to make my life seem more normal, or at the very least, less interesting.

I went about my day as usual, following my daily routines, trying to bring some stability back to my rocky life. From the outside, I appeared to have it all together. No one seemed to notice that I had been crying my eyes out night after night or that I had been suffering inside for months. They saw a beautiful woman with a lot going for her. They saw me as confident and outgoing and that was just how I wanted it. It was safer with people thinking all was well. If I appeared less vulnerable, there would be less chance of being taken advantage of. I had always envisioned myself as a strong woman, but I needed to prove to myself that I was indeed that person.

Lately I had been feeling weak inside. The single life for me was more lonely than exciting and it didn't suit me. Having been married for nearly half of my life, made my singleness that much lonelier. Although I was a virgin bride, married life meant a very active sex life. I often felt that my sex life with Kyle was the main reason we lasted 12 years. We didn't have a lot in common and sex was like the glue in our relationship. I always felt that Kyle did not love me as much as I loved him and that the only way to feel truly close to him was to engage in the most intimate act between husband and wife. It was the closest I could get to him and the only form of communication that we both seemed to understand. When we would argue, we would make up with sex; when we were happy, we'd show it with sex; and when we were bored or broke or both, we'd have sex. If we weren't having sex, I'd feel that there was trouble in our relationship, which is primarily why the end of our relationship took me by such surprise. Up until a shortly before he left, sex was good and I had no idea that he was unhappy. Even with the instances of phone sex that I had discovered, I had not suspected an impending affair. I always told him that if he ever had sex with another woman during our marriage, and then came back to my bed, that there would be dire consequences. I think even during his indiscretion, he at least respected that. He likely only refused my advances by concocting some excuse about an illness the week before he left me because he had already slept with Angela and he knew better than to sleep with me afterwards.

Now, I was lonely for not only companionship but for intimacy. I longed for the hands of a man to caress my body. This had been the longest that I had gone without sex since I was a teenage bride. It was as if I was boiling inside and I needed all the strength in my body to calm the fire. I avoided most contact with the men that were attracted to me at work for fear of making a hasty decision. There were at least a couple of men who I knew must be waiting for the right time to approach me. The gossip among the nurses was like wildfire, and it didn't take long to hear about who was after whom. Of course, I was the new divorcee and I was trying hard not to appear weak and vulnerable.

My workday had ended and I was leaving the building through a side entrance that was closer to my car. As I walked down the hall, I heard someone approaching from behind, almost like they were running. I didn't turn around until I heard my name in a deep sort of whisper.

"Maddie."

I turned around and saw Blake approaching me. I was a bit surprised because I hadn't really ever spoken to Blake. He was the hot guy everyone was after that I didn't have time for. I wondered what he wanted from me, but I expected it was the same as a lot of men lately. It was as though I carried a sign that said, "I'm divorced and haven't had sex in a long time, come and get me." It had caused me to develop a bit of an attitude towards men in general, but not so much that I had forgotten how much I desired one. I was beginning to wonder if I was developing the thinking of the typical man. While I once thought of sex as a romantic interlude between lovers, I was reaching the point where I could actually see myself engaging in sex just for pleasure.

Blake caught up to me and we were now face to face. He was a close talker, but I was not the type to step back when someone invaded my personal space. Quite the contrary, in general I would have stepped forward invading his as well, however, I sensed his closeness was not to intimidate me. He was very tall and I had to look up at his face at this close distance. He looked down at me with his stunning green eyes and asked me if he could walk me to my car. It seemed silly since I had walked myself to my car every other day, but it was obvious that he merely wanted to accompany me, so I obliged.

As we walked towards my car, he asked me what I did for fun. Figuring I'd scare him away for sure, I told him that the only fun I had time for was to hang out with my two little girls and play Nintendo with my three-year-old son. The comment didn't send him running. As I approached my car, I backed up against the door and as he reached for the door handle, his hand gently brushed against my side. With his hand still on the handle of my car door, he stood there in front of me and kicked a few pebbles around as he stared at the ground, not quite sure what to say next. Although I attempted to keep a nonchalant attitude, it became more difficult as he stepped closer to me and I raised my head to peer into his gorgeous green eyes. His eyes seemed to project warmth that perforated the soul. I shook my head as if to break the hypnotic state that he had put me in. He was standing so close that I could feel his breath as he asked me if he could take me somewhere sometime.

Somewhere, sometime... it seemed like a distant plan or promise that would never happen. It was easy to say yes, there was no commitment, no date, and no time, just somewhere, sometime.

"Sure," I said.

Still holding on to my door handle with his right hand, he placed his left hand on the car beside my face and stood there and looked at me for what seemed like a long time, but was probably more like a few seconds. Then he gently parted his lips and began to speak.

"Ok, so can I have your number?"

I gave him my number and he was gone as quickly as he'd arrived. There was something mysterious about him that I couldn't put my finger on at the moment. I stood there with my hand against the door handle and felt something deep inside the pit of my stomach, almost like butterflies. I was a grown woman and it couldn't be butterflies; I must have eaten something wrong for lunch. I was sure that it had nothing to do with the short and simple encounter with this tall, handsome physical therapist whose name sounded like a character from a daytime soap opera.

That evening after I put the kids to bed, I went back to my computer to escape to my secret world. There seemed to be so many directions that I could go and I wasn't sure which path to follow. I'd always been a firm believer that when one door closes another one opens, but there I was with a multitude of doors in front of me. Would I choose the correct one or would I enter the wrong one and only fall deeper into despair? My soul hungered for the answer, but I knew the only way to find out would be to take a chance and follow one of those paths.

Robert still wrote to me, and he felt that my place was with him. Greg wrote to me daily and my relationship with him was growing deeper. Dr. Marx was becoming friendlier every day and now I was confused by a brief encounter with a tall, handsome coworker who wanted to take me "somewhere, sometime." It seemed everywhere I turned there was an eligible bachelor trying to lure me in. I knew I wasn't ready. I was still in love with Kyle. I wondered if I would ever fall out of love with him. How would I love again if every passing moment was filled with memories of our marriage?

The last week of March passed quickly and I had a wonderful weekend with the kids. It was hard to believe it was already the beginning of a new week and I was back at work. Monday, April 1, 1996. Today was the day my divorce from Kyle was final. I had appeared in court with my attorney before coming to work and expected that Kyle would be there as well. To my surprise, he and his representation were both absent. Perhaps he didn't want to sit in the same room with me. He had already showed up at our mandatory parenting class for divorcing couples with children. The class was not easy for either of us; partly because it was difficult to be in the same room together and partly because with all the other divorcing couples gathered in the same room, the tenseness in the air was so thick you could cut it with a knife.

The counselor talked about how divorce is a major stress for families. He pointed out the facts and statistics and talked about how even years after a divorce, some parents continue to experience significant difficulties in coping and rebuilding their lives, mostly because of the inability to leave the past behind them. Even harder was listening to the statistics about the negative effects on children and how many of these effects follow them into adult-

◄ **BEYOND THE PRESENT**

hood. To think that my children's self-esteem and psychological adjustment could be impaired because of our divorce was hard to swallow. It was even more difficult knowing I had no choice in the matter. There was nothing I could do to change the inevitable.

Levi was only three. According to statistics, three-year-olds experience insecurity and feelings of being frightened during a divorce. They may experience nightmares, whining, crying, clinginess, tantrums, and even changes in eating and sleeping behaviors. Kaliegh was only eight and the statistics for her were not any better; trouble separating their own needs from those of their parents, feelings of sadness, loss, and uncertainty, anxiety, school problems, abandonment, anger and rejection, denial and self-blame. And then there was my Katy, who was almost 12 and would statistically experience similar feelings of loss and rejection, helplessness, loneliness, embarrassment, powerlessness, anger, tendencies to blame one parent, school problems, feelings of mixed loyalties, and depression. Listening to these statistics made me feel powerless myself. I realized that there was no way to prevent their suffering, just as there was no way to prevent my own. The only thing I could do was make sure that I watched for any of these symptoms and work hard to keep the communication open and help them to deal with the pain and loss they were experiencing. The support system that I had from the hospital I worked at was all that kept me sane, and I knew that I would have to be that support system for my kids.

My understanding was if you didn't show up in court for your final decree, anything could be granted and you might not have a say in the matter. I figured Kyle was confident that things would go according to the documentation and felt no need to show up for the occasion. The courtroom was mostly empty and the judge briefly reviewed the papers before asking me standard questions that had to do with changing my name. In a matter of minutes, the court entered my decree and I was single. I was granted managing conservatorship of the kids with the responsibility for making decisions regarding their health, education, where they would live and attend school, and moral and religious upbringing. Kyle was granted possessory conservator with similar rights while he was in possession of the kids during his visitation.

I had opted to drop my last name and use my first and middle name as my full legal name. I was an artist, and I already had a collection of paintings with my married name as the signature. I wanted to ensure that any paintings going forward would bear my own name. There was something different about being single and I experienced a feeling that I had not expected, a freedom that I had never felt before. At the same time, there was a panic inside, a rush of adrenaline, the understanding that the decisions I made going forward would be made alone and that I alone would bear the responsibility for the consequences of those decisions.

As I sat at my desk with the clock ticking nearer to time to go home, I scribbled my name on a piece of paper, minus the last name that I had used since I was 15. I wondered if the kids would be affected by my having a different last name than them, but quickly dismissed the concern. I would forever be "Mom" to them and my last name would surely have little significance on their ability to adjust. I thought about how today was April Fools' Day. Although there was surely some pagan origin for the traditions of making jokes on April 1st, I no longer considered myself a member of my previous religion, although I would forever identify myself as spiritual. Before my divorce from Kyle, I'd always had a great sense of humor. Growing up in a large family, you had to maintain a good sense of humor. But since my divorce, I was all too aware of the negativity and gloominess that seemed to be overtaking my lighthearted personality. I made a decision that I would reclaim that part of myself, and what better day to start than April Fools' Day! I picked up the phone and called Kyle.

"Hello."

"Hi Kyle, it's me Maddie... You didn't show up in court today and neither did your attorney."

"It's not required that I show up."

"No, I know... But since you weren't there, the judge made an amendment to your child support order and you have to pay $200 more per month than originally agreed upon."

"WHAT? You can't do that!"

I decided not to carry it out any further, since his first reaction was already enough for me to see that the joke worked.

"April Fools! Happy final divorce day!"

Kyle was very angry at this point. "Maddie, you think this is a big joke don't you? What is wrong with you? You are sick."

I was used to being labeled by Kyle. Being called sick, crazy, and psychotic were all too familiar to me. He often used these terms when he was angry with me. Perhaps his intent was to demean me or perhaps he really believed what he said. It didn't matter anymore and although I was confident in the condition of my mental stability, if I were sick or psychotic at this point in my life, I was sure it had everything to do with being married to him for 12 years. Emotionally on the other hand, I was sick, or perhaps a better description, wounded.

"Kyle, just because I am not your wife, just because you broke my heart, does not mean that you have broken me as a person. I am still Maddie and I still have the same sense of humor that I have always had. Why you think you are powerful enough to change me is beyond my understanding, but I won't change because of you!"

Kyle hung up the phone without another word spoken. I was shaken a little; I was pretty sure that my joke would not be found funny in Kyle's eyes. I wasn't sure why I felt the need to make the call. I always believed that "humor is where the heart is." Maybe if I joked about our situation and found the humor in things that were otherwise not funny at all, perhaps my heart would follow and the anger that had built up inside of me and the pain that had come from that anger would melt away and be replaced with a less burdensome sense of humor. I decided that this phone call was proof that our relationship was irreconcilable. Not that I had ever been given any other indication, but my hopes that one day Kyle and I could be civil to each other and share the parenting of our children with at least a sense of mutual respect was more than likely doomed.

CHAPTER 9

Selling The House

The winter had faded and I had listed my house for sale. I decided that I could no longer live in this small town. There were too many memories and too many lost friends. I could not escape from people who knew me when I was little or even worse, when I was married. I needed to start a new life in a new town. My relationship with Greg had flourished and our talks had become more intimate. We shared so much and he swore he was falling in love with me. I didn't believe in love at the time. I had experienced my one love and felt that there was no second chance. Perhaps I'd find a partner or companion, but I had lost the hope of ever finding another love. Love and marriage had lost the meaning it once had for me and I felt like I had lost a sense of innocence with the serving of the divorce papers. It had become all too clear how easily something I once held sacred could so quickly be ended. A piece of paper and a judge, a couple signatures, and a few months later you are single. All the hard work and effort to keep a marriage going for 12 long years, the loyalty, faithfulness, nothing matters as soon as one partner wants out. It's over as quickly as it began.

None-the-less, California was where I had always thought Kyle and I would move, and since Greg lived there, it seemed like a comfortable choice. I wasn't sure how fast my house would sell, so I continued to try and keep our schedules as normal as possible. It was difficult, being a single mother, to schedule showings of the house. I had opted to sell by owner. There would be no money to move to California if I had to pay realtor's fees. I was confident in my abilities and had found a local mortgage and title company that would help me work out the details. The house was in my name, as was everything else that Kyle turned his back on. Even full custody of the children was an easy exchange for my willingness to accept the large hospital bills we had racked up over the years because we were without insurance. For me there was no question, I knew I would eventually want to move and the only way I could do so was if I had controlling custody of the kids. I did not earn very much as a secretary. I had resolved myself to making minimum payments on the hospital bills for as long as it took. More importantly, there would be no custody battle.

 It was Friday afternoon and I had scheduled a showing of the house at 4 p.m. I arranged for my mother to watch the kids so the house would be empty. I needed it to be in pristine condition for the best impression possible. I paced the living room waiting for the arrival of the potential buyers. I was nervous, since I had made a firm decision and knew that selling this house was a vital step towards the lengthy process of shaping my future. I paced the floor with my arms clenched tightly around my waist. I caught a glimpse of myself in the mirror. I hardly noticed my own reflection as I used my finger to rub the smudge off the mirror. I stepped back and surveyed the reflection of the carefully placed furniture in my living room. There were many memories that I would leave behind in this former home that now just seemed like a shrine of reminders of human failure. I knew that any pleasant thoughts and recollections of this home would fade as the love I shared with Kyle became buried under the new future that I would create. I knew that Levi would have no memory of this house or the home that we had created as a family. I wondered what future of mine would turn out to be his childhood memories, and I feared that I would make the wrong choices and leave shards of broken memories and heartache in his past. It was hard enough to accept the damage that Kyle had already done and to see the pain that my children suffered as we struggled to make separate lives.

It was a quarter past four when the doorbell rang. Although I was expecting it to ring, it caught me by surprise. As I opened the door, I saw two well-dressed gentlemen with friendly faces. The taller of the two was an older gentleman with a receding hairline. The other was a handsome, younger man with a mustache. He had wavy brown hair and it was he who greeted me with a handshake.

"You must be Madeline, I'm Nick and this is my brother Jack."

"Yes, I'm Madeline, nice to meet you both, please come in."

I was obviously nervous as they entered my house. I felt as though my life was about to be scrutinized. Lucky for me, they were only interested in my home and not my life. The grand tour of my humble abode took little time. It was a small, 3 bedroom, 2 bath, older home with a somewhat country charm. It was a simple home for a once simple life. Little did these two strangers know that my life was much more complicated now. They were both very friendly and they both seemed excited about my house and I was sure that they would submit an offer. They asked many questions: Would I consider leaving the washer and dryer? Did the wall heater work? I was as accommodating as possible, and Nick handed me his card as I escorted them out.

Only three days had passed when I received a phone call from Nick. He was very friendly and explained that he and his brother would like to make and offer on my home. They wanted to purchase it as an investment and use it as a rental. We discussed the details and the offer was reasonable. They agreed to allow me an extra long escrow and to rent the house until I was ready to move. We made arrangements to meet at the title company and put the terms in writing. Nick was very matter of fact in his tone, and I sensed nothing other than a businessman in his dealings with me. However, that all changed after our meeting at the title company. Although the meeting went smoothly and the offer was solid, I was taken by surprise as I was leaving the building. Nick approached me and requested to take me to dinner that evening. I politely declined because I had the kids during the week, but accepted for the coming weekend. I was a bit surprised, not by the invitation, but by my acceptance. I thought to myself as I was leaving, at least the deal is done and there are no strings attached. Still, I was nervous. Sure I had met Robert online and traveled to Tennessee, and I had accepted a "somewhere, sometime" invitation from Blake, but I had not accepted a true "date" until now. My divorce was barely final, and I was an emotionally driven, lonely, sex-starved basket case. I knew that I had no business accepting this date. I was not sure if I had accepted out of a true desire for adult companionship or for the fact that he had just bought my house. In either case, the date was set and I fully intended to go through with it.

The week became even more complicated when I arrived at work on Wednesday morning to find a voicemail from Dr. Marx. It was yet another invitation to dinner. I was beginning to wonder if I looked hungry. I was hungry for sure, but the craving that I experienced was of another kind. I had a yearning for intimacy and this basic animal magnetism was obviously attracting the opposite sex no matter how much I tried to hide it.

I confided with one of my favorite nurses about the invitation from Dr. Marx. I shared openly knowing that it was only a matter of time before it was public knowledge. Either it would become public because Dr. Marx would confide in one of the nurses, who would then share with her friends, or because I was sharing with my own friends. In either case, nothing remained private once shared inside the walls of the hospital. Even doctor-patient confidentiality was difficult to protect. It was as if there were notes or files for every personal life within the walls of the rehab hospital and it only took opening a couple to overturn the many secrets hiding inside. That was the reason I chose to decline Dr. Marx's invitation. I knew whatever happened between us would not be private. Not to mention, my supervisor, Kay, reminded me that it was not permitted for Dr. Marx to date me. She was noticeably upset that he had even asked. I'm sure that this was triggered by her deep concern for me and having supported me through this most difficult time of my life; she was one of the few people that I trusted and merely wanted to protect me. I knew that Kay would not have objected if I had insisted on dating him. But, she was a true friend and I didn't want to put her in that position.

By Saturday, I was almost ready to cancel my date with Nick. I was sure that it was a mistake, but there was something pushing me to go through with it. I think inside I still needed to avenge myself after Kyle had hurt me so deeply. I wished that somehow Kyle would know I was going on this date, and even more so, I wished that he cared.

I sat down at my computer to check my email. My inbox was full as usual, a typical email from Robert, an email from Greg asking where I had been and stating how much he missed me on chat, and then my heart skipped a beat as I noticed a reply from Angela. I remembered sending the email informing her of how badly she had hurt our family by sleeping with Kyle. I was afraid to open the email. Thoughts flooded my mind. I knew she would not admit to her indiscretion and I was sure that even if she did I would only hate her more. I couldn't just sit and look at the unopened email. I had to open it, and when I did it was just as I figured. She insisted how sorry she was and that Kyle had sworn to her that he was single. I doubted her story and just as I thought, I hated her more. She explained how she was a public official and would not have slept with a married man intentionally. I didn't believe her and I didn't care. I hated that I opened the email. It was like pouring salt on an open wound. Reading the words in the email, I pictured her typing them with the same fingers that caressed my husband's body. The anger boiled inside me and I was driven even more to go through with my date with Nick.

The evening was warm for early spring, and I picked a sexy, short dress for my date night. I spent an hour preparing. Not that it took an hour to dress and put on my make-up, but it took a good hour to muster up the nerve to go out with Nick in the first place. I felt that awkward feeling that I often got when I knew I was about to make a mistake. I was angry inside, fueled with the latest email from Angela, and it was obvious that it was a bad decision to go out with Nick in my state of mind. His arrival time was nearing and I knew there was no turning back. The bell rang and I opened the door half eagerly and half dreadfully. Nick was a perfect gentleman. He drove to the restaurant, opened the doors for me, pulled out my chair, and laughed at my jokes. However, there was something secretive about him. He hardly spoke a word on our date. I was already outgoing and being around the silent type made me even more talkative. By the end of our date, he was as much a stranger to me as he was at the beginning, but he was extremely handsome and there was definitely chemistry between us.

After dinner, Nick drove me back to my house. I had consumed a bit more wine than my body could process in such a short time and I was beginning to feel the effects. I was sure that to Nick I was an easy target. But deep down, I knew that was exactly what I intended to be. The alcohol merely paved the way for what was about to happen and made it easier to clear my conscience and enjoy myself. He walked me to my door and just like he surely expected, I pulled him inside and closed the door behind us. I never turned on the light and we barely made it past the first piece of furniture before we landed on the sofa. Nick had obviously expected the occasion as he conveniently carried protection. There was barely time to use it. It was a ravenous frenzy and we ripped at each other's clothing as if driven by some temporary madness. It was only minutes before our naked bodies were united as one. The strength of his toned body rising and falling above me, the smell of his cologne, combined with the alcohol on his breath, was like a storm that rushed through my body. I quivered intensely.

But just as quickly as the storm arrived, the weather changed. There was not a word exchanged between us and barely a glance. We were just two lonely people with basic human needs willing to sacrifice our bodies for a moment of passion. As he reached for his shirt, I pulled myself up behind his back and as my breast brushed against his smooth skin, I gently whispered in his ear, "Don't call me." I'm sure he had no intention of calling me, but if I were to tell him not to call then I would have control of the situation. I knew that in a strange way I used him as much as he used me. I longed for the physical release that he provided me. But no matter how good the sex, it would never mean as much as making love to Kyle. So I made sure it didn't matter at all.

CHAPTER **10**

Changes

Spring had officially arrived, the air was beginning to warm and flowers had already begun to bloom. I continued on a day-to-day basis to try and put Kyle behind me. But, as soon as I thought I had forgotten that I had gone through a divorce, I would turn the corner and quickly be reminded when I would see families together or couples holding hands. What would have normally gone unnoticed now stood out like a huge flashing sign that said, "Maddie is alone." I tried to console myself by thinking of how lucky I was to be a mother and to have three beautiful, healthy children. Even with the laughter and joy that motherhood brought, my children could not fill the loneliness that was deep inside of me. I was certain after my experience with Nick that not even a man could fill this loneliness. This was a loneliness brought about by a loss, similar to the grief of losing a loved one to death itself. I had previously experienced death in my family, and the break-up of my marriage left an all too familiar emptiness in my heart. This was an empty space in my chest; a space with Kyle's name on it that would forever remain his space. I had to find a way to forget the pain that existed deep within me. I was convinced it was going nowhere and the only way to stop feeling it was to occupy my time in some other way.

    I devoted my time to entertaining the kids during the weekends they were with me. We went to minor league baseball games, shopped at the mall, played at the parks, and spent time making crafts and painting pictures. I had been an artist since I was a teenager and every passing year my talent seemed to grow. I enjoyed painting because it allowed me to escape from reality. I could sit and paint a picture and hours would pass when it felt like only minutes. I always encouraged the kids to be creative, and already I could see Katy blossoming as a young artist. She had a skill that even I did not possess. I could copy any drawing or photograph but Katy would create art from her own incredible imagination.

One Saturday afternoon the kids and I decided to search for a place to take photographs so I could paint their portrait. We piled in the car and drove about 10 miles out of town where there were only fields of brush and cattle. We didn't have to drive much further when we came upon an old broken down barn with a windmill. We pulled off the side of the road and climbed the fence to check out our discovery. The barn was old and falling apart, but a few walls still stood and there were piles of straw, an old hay rack, and a feed trough, which turned out to be a gold mine for an artist. I never considered myself to be a photographer, but having an eye for art meant knowing a good place to take a photograph. I could envision my painting even before I took the picture. This was a perfect spot and I took approximately 100 photographs while we were there. The sky began to turn orange and the wind started to pick up. You could see a storm brewing in the distance, so we hurried to finish up, grabbed a few rocks as souvenirs, and then we scurried to the car to beat the storm.

My time with the kids was valuable and I knew that they needed these outings even more than I did. They needed to feel important in my life even though my divorce consumed so much of my energy. Even when I was home with them, I knew they could sense my mental distraction.

The day had been such a great escape and for once I was

able to forget about the pain of being single and focus on something I loved dearly, my beautiful children and my passion for art. I was excited and motivated to paint their portrait; however, I knew that this time my desire to paint was more than a tool to pass the time, and more than the simple pleasure of doing something I loved. The portrait I would paint would be significant in my healing process. I would be creating with my own hands a surviving memorial of our tragic past and I knew in my heart that the photos I had taken that evening were going to be the beginning of a masterpiece. With the unveiling of the art piece, this tragedy would be replaced with a beautiful likeness of the most precious result of the relationship that I had built with Kyle over the past 12 years.

That evening when the kids were tucked quietly into bed, I crept down the hall to my secret online world where I welcomed the adult conversation almost nightly. When I shared the story of our photography session with Greg, he was very excited. He too loved to take photographs, especially of his children. Greg made it clear that he felt something very special for me. He knew I would be moving to California and he envisioned us together in the future. I had never met him face to face and if I learned nothing else from Robert, I learned that just because you have a great relationship by email or chat it does not mean there will be chemistry once you meet in person. I was a little uneasy about meeting him face to face, but there was a certain comfort level in feeling like I had already made a friend in the place I would soon call home.

I made my decision and my choice was Sacramento, California. Greg liked to think it was because he was located only 20 miles away, but there was plenty of work in Sacramento and I had already lined up a temporary agency to help me find employment. The pay scale was much higher in California than it was in this small West Texas town, partially due to the high cost of living. It would be a struggle to live there, but I was already accustomed to struggling and by moving, I felt sure that I would eliminate many other stresses in my life. Maybe I was trying to run away from my troubles. There were times when I asked myself if that was the case, but it was easier to run than to stay and face the issues. In a way, I was taking the path of least resistance; however, ironically, the path I chose was very difficult. I often thought about how, by moving, I was adding another enormous life changing event to my already stressful life. Each time I would speak to Greg, he would try to pin me down to a date to fly out and meet him. I would avoid the subject as much as possible, since my life was already complicated by work, single motherhood, and the many male distractions that constantly surrounded me. I knew that Greg thought he was the only male contact in my life and I did nothing to convince him otherwise, but in reality, he was just one of many.

When I was home, I screened my calls and seldom picked up the phone. I had messages at the end of every workday. Most of the calls were from men that I had known all my life or firefighters that worked with Kyle. I avoided them like the plague, since I was never sure of their intent. Perhaps Kyle had put them up to calling me so he could trap me. In fact, most of the phone calls from men went unreturned. I was amazed at how much attention I received when all I really wanted was Kyle back in my life. Even that was ironic because I was still very angry with Kyle, and after what he had done, I knew I could never forgive him. I wanted him back in my life but I wanted things back the way they were before Angela, before our computer, before the pain. I knew at this point he was not coming back and I would have to move beyond him, and I wondered if another man would perhaps allow me just enough distraction to forget how much I missed my former life. Greg was there for conversation, but I still craved the physical contact that he could not provide from afar. Nick was not an option; he had fulfilled his purpose. He was like a sacrifice to cover the sin that Kyle had committed against me.

For now I felt free. Free to be with whomever I chose, and I no longer considered myself the innocent victim of circumstance.

I thought about Blake and his invitation to take me "somewhere, sometime." I thought about his mysterious demeanor and his deep, sexy voice. I wondered why he had not called me and if he was intimidated by me. For now, I had other things to keeping me busy; paintings, my outings with the kids, and conversations with Greg. But these were only temporary diversions and would not indefinitely suppress my physical desires.

I was still engaged in idle chat with Greg when a stranger's window popped up on my screen. A man named Charles asking questions about me. I had all the online friends I could handle at the moment and tried to avoid conversation with him. And then I noticed he was from my hometown and it struck my curiosity. We started to chat and then he asked if I was single, which had become the most common question on chat forums. I mentioned that I had just gone through a divorce. I told him that my ex had dumped me for a woman online and that she swore he told her he was single. It was easy to share. It was as if each time that I mentioned my circumstance, I would begin to accept it just a little bit more. Surprisingly, he asked me if my ex was a firefighter.

"Yes, how did you know?"

"I was just guessing... I chatted with a woman recently who told me the other side of the story, something about how she met a firefighter in my hometown and he told her he was single but he turned out to be married."

I was sure this was some sort of setup! Could it be possible he was telling the truth? I was still desperately looking for closure and there were so many unanswered questions. If Angela had actually spoken to this man and told him that Kyle stated he was single, then possibly some of the anger that I carried towards her could melt away and I'd be one step closer to being free from the pain that the anger inside of me was causing. Or, would I merely transfer the anger that I had towards her onto Kyle until it consumed me like a burning inferno deep in my soul? I continued to probe him with questions.

"I can't answer all these questions on chat... I don't type as fast as you do. Since we both live in the same town, why don't we meet up for drinks and discuss the situation?"

I so intensely wanted my questions answered that I almost, without hesitation, responded with a "Yes." But then, there was the little person inside me who stepped up to remind me of how wrong I had been in my choice to meet Robert. Not that anything bad had come out of meeting him; however, the fact that it could have had dire consequences could not escape my thoughts. What if this was a serial killer who picked up women he met on chat?

"I'll think about it... I'm not sure I want to meet someone else from chat in person."

"Someone else?"

"Yes, been there done that, it didn't work out so well."

"Ok... it's just for drinks and conversation.. but suit yourself. I'll be here tomorrow night if you change you mind."

For the rest of the evening, my thoughts were consumed with the potential answers I could receive from this man I briefly met on chat. However, I knew that much of what I came across on chat was hardly as it seemed. The very fact that I was actually chatting with a man was questionable. This internet chat thing was so new, and even with all that I had been through over the last few months, I was still quick to trust the letters that moved across my screen as fact. I had to remind myself that the entire thing could be dangerous. Although it appeared to be merely entertainment, it was all too obvious now how simple conversation could lead to something much more real. But this late in the game, all the reasoning in the world didn't change the fact that I needed or wanted answers to questions that were probably better left unasked, and it was only a matter of time before my longing for understanding would get the best of me and I'd meet yet another stranger in a futile attempt to sort out my pain.

Lately, my Saturday nights were spent on the computer until the wee hours of the morning, so it was typical for me to sleep in on Sundays. However, sleeping in only consisted of staying in bed until I was awakened by a loud, repetitive knock on my door by one of my children with the promise they would surely starve to death if I didn't jump out of bed immediately to feed them. Typically, my nocturnal siestas were brief and lasted no later than 9:30 a.m., no matter what time I went to bed the previous night. For most of my life, Sunday mornings had been filled with the chaotic rush of trying to find dresses, socks, ties, and books in order to make it out the door in time so we didn't show up late for our Sunday church service.

It was 7:00 a.m. on Sunday, and this Sunday morning was entirely different. After my chat session with this stranger in my hometown who offered to meet me and share information that he had gathered from "the other woman," sleep was not an easy accomplishment. Most of the night, I tossed and turned and the only thing that slightly resembled sleep were the brief lapses into a familiar twilight dream state. I had always been a light sleeper and waking up and going to sleep all night seemed to keep me in a constant state of dreaming ever since I was a child. Oftentimes, I felt that these dreams were given to me to help me sort out my issues or solve difficult problems. Sometimes, I would awaken in the middle of the night with a poem in my head that I had to jot down or a plan that would get me out of bed and into my office to put it into action. Sleeping had always seemed like a waste of time to me and I was sure it was a symptom of my type-A personality. My motto, after all, was "I'll sleep when I die." So that particular Sunday morning, as I lay in bed at 7:00 a.m., even though I slept very little if any, I was wide awake. My mind raced with what-ifs and whys. What if I did meet with Charles? Why did he contact me? What information did he really have? Did I need to know?

But there was another subject that weighed heavily on my mind. It was painfully obvious that my children were aware of our Sunday morning change in routine. I had been stalling with the true answers to their questions as to why we were not going to church.

BEYOND THE PRESENT

This was such a difficult subject for me. Not only had I turned my back on the only religion I had ever known, I felt that my religion had turned its back on me. My religion had been engrained in me from such an early age and it had become so deep-seated that it was difficult for me to leave no matter how betrayed I felt. The guilt was overwhelming at times. I had never celebrated a single holiday or birthday and I had raised my children the same way. Now that I was sure I could no longer associate myself with this organization, how would I explain this to my children? I had taught them all of their lives how the holiday celebrations and birthdays were pagan and not to be celebrated by Christians. I once actually believed that my religious upbringing would protect me and that somehow merely being a member of the congregation meant that I would have a happy marriage and perfect children. But deep in my heart, I was not convinced that these teachings were correct and now that my life had been shattered by divorce, everything that I had been taught I now questioned.

Levi was too small to understand any of this, but somehow, I would have to face my daughters and do my best to explain in simple terms that Mommy has had a change of heart. I wasn't sure if they would embrace the thought of celebrating the holidays or if they would feel the guilt that plagued me. I sometimes feared that my eternal soul was at stake. Most of the time, I was able to logically accept that the only reason I ever believed the teachings that I was raised by were because it was the only life I had ever known. But sometimes the thoughts would enter my mind… "What if they are right?" "What if I have given up any chance for eternal life by separating myself from this organization?" In either case, I could no longer be a part of something that I did not believe in my heart. This group of people that were my only support system shunned me when I needed them most. I was convinced that this was not the Christian way and I would have to help my children gradually separate themselves from identifying with this group. I knew this would be difficult because even though Kyle had initiated the break-up of our family, he remained a part of this religion. Although I knew that Kyle didn't practice the strict side of our religion within the home during our marriage, it was important to him to be viewed by others in the congregation as spiritually strong. He would surely attempt to keep our children on that path and I feared how they would be affected by our contradictory teachings. I would have to be careful and allow my children to develop an independent way of thinking as they matured. No matter what happened in my future, it was that morning as I lay in bed that I firmly decided that I would never force a religious viewpoint on my children. I decided that instead of springing my decision on the girls that I would talk to them the next time they asked me why we were not going to church. I didn't know then that I would be having this conversation in just a few hours on that very day.

It was after lunch and the girls were playing with their Barbies quietly in their bedroom. Meanwhile, Levi pushed his toy fire truck up and down the hall, squealing with excitement and using every bit of his little lung capacity to replicate the high pitched sounds of the siren. Normally, I would have tried to quiet him as I lay on my bed for a moment of afternoon peace, but this time, I felt a sense of comfort in knowing that, for the moment, my little boy could escape into his fantasy world where firemen were actually heroes and not daddies who left mommies. As I thumbed through the pages of a magazine, a gloomy faced Kaliegh greeted me.

"What's the matter?" I asked.

"How come we don't go to church anymore?"

It had happened. The dreaded question that I knew would come up sooner or later. The very question I had pondered when I woke this morning. I called Katy and Levi into my bedroom. If I was going to have the dreaded discussion, I needed to make sure they were all together so I would only have to do this one time. Typically, I've always been the type to over communicate, even with the kids, and this time was no different. It probably would have sufficed to say something simple and to the point, like, "Mommy doesn't believe in our religion anymore so we are not going to church," but I felt the need to make sure that they fully understood my reasoning and that I kept their attention long enough to receive their feedback. It was important to me to hear how my decision affected them even though I knew that I would not change my mind. I felt sure that although my decision was a difficult one to make, it would in some sense free them from the pain that I had suffered growing up in this religion. I also knew that this would not be without some initial discomfort for them and possibly some guilt as we transitioned into a family that we would have, at one time, shunned.

My explanation was brief but thorough. I was careful to explain that the only reason that I had followed our religion was because it was all that I had been taught and how other people have been taught differently and they live according to their beliefs. I explained that I had not decided exactly what my own beliefs were, but that I did not believe that celebrating holidays would make us bad people and if anything, it would bring us closer together. Katy's eyes beamed with excitement. She was having a difficult time containing this excitement and immediately broke out in conversation filled with supporting excuses about how my choice was the best choice and how she never understood anyway and could hardly wait until the next holiday so she could be a full participant! Levi didn't really have a full understanding of what I was saying until he heard Katy and watched her practically jump up and down with excitement, and then of course as soon as he heard the word "party," he was sure that we were discussing something wonderful. While Katy and Levi held hands and jumped for joy, I turned to Kaliegh expecting to receive a similar response, but instead there was a quite unexpected reaction. As I looked at her, I could see her eyes filling with tears. Kaliegh had never been good with change, and whether a positive or negative change, it was still a change. Her life was best left undisrupted. The tears streamed down her face and I will never forget the words that came out of her mouth.

She calmly and tearfully uttered the words, "But won't God be angry at us?"

Why should I have expected anything different? For years both Kyle and I had been teaching her what we had been taught by our parents; the interpretation of the scriptures by a religious organization who was actually in the minority as far as interpretations go. Virtually all other religions celebrate at least some form of the various holidays. But we had worked hard to instill the belief that God did not want us to participate in these pagan holiday celebrations. Now, I was "changing my mind." Understanding how difficult this must have been for her having to already endure such great changes in her life with Mommy and Daddy living separately, I could do nothing more than to pull her close to me and hold her as I stroked her hair. I explained that she never had to do anything that made her feel uncomfortable and I promised her that as long as she wanted to abstain from celebrating her birthday, Christmas, Easter, Valentine's Day, or any other holiday, that she would not be pressured by anyone to do so.

Katy tried to help comfort Kaliegh, but I knew that Kaliegh and I were very much alike, and I knew that deep down, no matter how much I tried to make her feel like we were a team, that she felt very alone inside. No matter how mixed up I was when it came to religion, I still believed there was a God in heaven, and I prayed for Kaliegh first knowing that while she tried to appear to be the strong one, she was very fragile. It was times like these that I found being a mother so challenging. I would ask myself all the time, have I just said or done something that will negatively impact my child's future? It's a very intense and scary feeling to know that every decision you make and every time you open your mouth to speak to your children, you are in some way shaping their future, be it good or bad. But for that moment, I only knew what was in my heart and I truly believed that the choice I was making would have a positive effect on their lives.

Katy was wise beyond her years emotionally speaking, and

we exchanged a sort of glance that without verbally communicating, clearly stated that the holiday subject would remain sensitive and would not be joyfully shared in front of Kaliegh until enough time would pass that Kaliegh would be comfortable or accept the changes in our lives. Fortunately, it would be many months before we would be discussing the celebration of a birthday, and the holidays were even further away. We all tried to put the holiday conversation behind us for the rest of the afternoon. I did my best to hug Kaliegh as often as possible that day to silently reassure her that I was on her side and that things would be okay.

CHAPTER **11**

A Need To Know

The weekend had been very emotional for all of us and I spent the following week trying hard to focus on the kids, almost ignoring my secret online life. But by the time the week was over and Kyle whisked the kids away for their weekend "party," I felt myself longing for that online connection as though it were some sort of electronic addiction. I referred to Kyle's weekends with the kids as a party because, in my opinion, Kyle spent every moment with the kids trying to glamorize the fact that he now lived separate from us, lavishing the kids with gifts and indulging them with ice-cream treats and outings at the park, all of the things that he rarely involved himself in during our together times. I can't say I totally blamed him for this, doing so would obviously make the kids more excited to see Daddy and less aware of the fact that they were now part of a broken home. Sometimes I worried that they wouldn't want to come home since my house was the place where all the mundane parts of their lives existed; going to school, cleaning their room, and doing homework. Even worse, it was the place where memories of our family as it existed in the past flourished only to be confronted with the realization that our lives were much different now. Visiting Daddy was more like a vacation where our broken home could be left behind.

It was Friday evening and at least the kids weekend with Dad allowed me to catch up on emails. There were emails from Greg about his kids and the weather in California, asking when I would be willing to fly out and meet him, emails from Robert asking why I seemed to be ignoring him, and messages from other insignificant internet relationships that I had forged in a futile attempt to step outside of the chaos called my life. I had been thinking a lot about whether or not to meet with Charles to discuss what he knew about Kyle and Angela. Part of me figured he probably didn't know anything more than I already knew and I'm sure there was a part of me that was just curious to meet this stranger that seemed to care about my situation. Sometimes I wanted to escape from my life and never talk about my divorce or my pain again, and yet in some strange way it was actually comforting to tell my story to others. Perhaps sharing my story prompted sympathy, which actually made me feel better for the moment. It was 6 p.m. and I logged onto my computer and wasn't surprised that Charles was there. It was almost as if these strangers actually lived inside my computer and at any moment I could just flip a switch and they would be there for me to chat with. However, I seemed to have a problem keeping them inside this box that sat on my desk. Here I was again, typing words across the screen and making arrangements to meet Charles at a bar downtown, a bar actually called "The Bar." Charles described how he looked and what he would be wearing and I described how I looked and the sexy, white dress that I would have on. In only a couple of hours, I'd be meeting a total stranger in a bar. I was not the bar type and during my entire 12 year relationship with Kyle, I think I had only been to a bar maybe once or twice. I despised cigarette smoke and generally despised the crowd that hung out at these establishments. This time I had a purpose, or at least I convinced myself that I had a purpose. I often wondered what it was that gave me the courage to meet total strangers in unfamiliar surroundings. I am not sure if it was an overwhelming curiosity or a deep internal desire to rebel after being so good all of my life. Although I had an occasional thought of "I hope this guy isn't some crazy person," there was not any "real" fear involved. It was only after the experiences were over that I would get a sense of how something horrible could have happened. Most of all, I think that I was truly lonely and taking that chance on a stranger was better than sitting at home alone.

It was time to get ready and I dug through my closet for the sexy, white dress that I had described to Charles. I didn't have many sexy outfits. Being part of a strict religious upbringing and being married to Kyle, the jealous type, made it difficult to dress sexy. I grabbed my short white dress that was cut high enough above the knee to show off my long, slender legs. I wasn't planning on seducing Charles that night, but dressing sexy always seemed to elicit the same response that I had become accustomed to when discussing the breakup of my marriage. It was a common statement: "He's crazy for leaving a woman as gorgeous as you." Somehow, it's often assumed that if a man cheats on his wife that his wife must be some hideous, old bag. Although it was painfully obvious to me by now that there is more to a marriage than two good-looking people, it was still comforting to me to hear that comment. Dressing sexy also made me feel wanted, although deep down I still craved being wanted by Kyle even though he wouldn't see me that night or know how I looked, or whom I was talking to. Even more painful was the thought that he wouldn't even care if he did. Still, there was a sense of control in being able to get a reaction out of strange men, knowing that I could decide if and when I would take it to the next level. I didn't have a lot of control over the rest of my life, so even the smallest feeling of control was cherished.

It was chilly out and being dressed in my slinky, short dress probably made me stand out even more. The cold was worth enduring as long as I looked hot. Hot enough to make any single man wish he were my husband. When I arrived at The Bar, there was very little parking. The building was small and old and was centered right downtown between several large commercial buildings. The already small parking lot was packed with cars and I was forced to park down the street and walk in the cold with my 3-inch high heels and bare legs. I was nervous about meeting a stranger, but maybe even more nervous knowing what the topic of conversation would be. When I reached the entrance, even before entering, I could smell cigarette smoke. I covered my mouth with both hands and took a large breath. My hands were cold and my breath warmed them slightly. I opened the door and entered The Bar. The place was filled with noise and there were TVs placed around on the walls all displaying various sporting events. The area seemed more cramped than I expected. There was a long strip of booths along one wall with a very narrow space between the booths and the bar. I gazed at the faces in the booths to see if could find someone that was watching for me. In the second to the last booth, I spotted a man fitting the description that Charles gave me. Our eyes locked and he looked surprised as he stood up and stepped out of the booth. The place was small but crowded, and although the bar was filled with voices, laughter, and the sound of sports on the TV's, I could hear his voice as he called my name with sort of a questioning tone and raised his hand as if to wave me his direction. I worked my way through the crowd of people loitering near the entrance of the bar and between the tables. Charles remained standing, and as I walked up to the booth, he extended his hand. His handshake was firm and his hand was as warm as his smile. He had sandy blonde hair with a mustache and glasses and although his physic was that of a younger man, I could see by the lines in his face that he was somewhere between 40 and 50. By his dress and overall demeanor, he appeared more professional, and perhaps more gentle than I had envisioned. Somehow, I pictured a rugged cowboy type, although living in West Texas made that the most likely type to expect. As I fully expected, his first comment was about how beautiful I was followed by the expected, "Wow, your husband must be crazy" comment. I guess my dress had done its job; here was another man pointing out how unfortunate my breakup was for Kyle. I grinned bashfully as if to be flattered by the comment, but in reality it was just another reminder of the fact that no matter how beautiful I was, Kyle did not want to be married to me.

It was no surprise to me when Charles explained how he really didn't know any more than he had shared with me in the chat forum, and how he was merely interested in meeting me because he felt that I was a fascinating woman. While Charles offered to buy me a drink, I politely refused, since I would have to drive myself home. While wine had become a great friend to me lately, I had learned too many lessons recently and I was careful not to drink when I was solely responsible for my children or when I was alone with a man I didn't know. It was easy to refrain from alcohol when I had my kids, but I knew that I was capable of breaking that rule when it came to men. We spent about a half hour talking about my situation as I drank my soda and he drank his beer. I realized that this meeting was not going to end like I had hoped. I was not going to have an eye opening revelation about Angela and Kyle. And to be honest, there was probably no more information to be discovered. He lied to me and he slept with her. How much more information did I really need?

I decided it was time to go, but Charles insisted I stay a bit longer. He didn't want to let me go. He was worried this would be the last time he would see me, and it was obvious to me even before he mentioned it that he was interested in seeing me again. I insisted that it was late and that the cigarette smoke was bothering me so I had to leave. Charles reached across the table and gently put his hand on my wrist, "Let's go for a short drive and get away from the smoke so we can talk somewhere quiet." Why would I go for a drive with this man who was only 40 minutes ago merely a conversation on my computer? I hesitated and for reasons unbeknownst even to me, I accepted. I wondered even then if perhaps I had a hunger for danger having been sheltered first by my parents and then by my religion. Was I now tempted to live on the edge, taking risks over and over again to somehow live like I assumed that others lived? But how sheltered was I? After all, it was my parents who allowed me to marry at the very young age of 15. It was I who accepted. Had this reckless lifestyle actually been a part of me all along? For as long as I can remember, I've taken chances. Yet even taking chances, I had always had the tendency to trust my instinct, and for some reason, this man seemed safe.

We left The Bar and headed towards the parking lot. As we approached Charles' car, it was immediately apparent that he wasn't hurting for money. He drove a newer model Mercedes 4-door coupe with a sliding glass sunroof. He rushed ahead of me to open the passenger door. It was even chillier outside than it was when I had arrived. He started the car and backed out of the parking lot. Initially, there was almost an eerie quiet. Neither of us spoke. His mobile phone rang and he took the call. His voice was soft and he didn't really say much to the person on the other end other than yes, no, uh huh, and maybe. I wondered if he was speaking to a man or a woman, maybe a girlfriend. It seemed rude to ask so I didn't. We drove down the street and about five minutes down the road, we were already out of the downtown area when we turned off towards an open field. I was a bit concerned about where we were going, and I used my usual technique of open and honest questions with a hint of laughter. Using humor and sarcasm was the best way I knew how to ask a difficult question, not wanting to appear truly afraid. But as the old saying goes, "humor is from the heart."

"Are you taking me to a vacant field to rape and kill me?"

He laughed out loud as he pulled the car over and parked by a massive drilling rig. He looked across the car at me and I immediately felt safe and calm. His eyes were warm and his gaze was endearing. He was definitely not a serial killer. We talked about his job as a drilling engineer and his past military service; we talked about my failed marriage and my plans to move to

California. I was careful not to mention my kids. It was my goal to make sure that the kids were completely separate from my dating life. I didn't want them to meet any of my new male friends. There was no need to involve them since I knew that all of these men who were merely distractions would be temporary in my life, and I knew that my kids needed stability and consistency.

Before he drove me back to The Bar, he reached out and touched my face with his hand. He whispered to me that I was special and he wished me well. I could see in his eyes that he wanted me. I wasn't interested in another one-night-stand, but I was pleased that I had met such a genuine person. He was kind and I sensed that although he would have had sex with me given the chance, he really meant what he said. We exchanged phone numbers and promised to keep in touch. We had already gone beyond the chat relationship and he was someone that I wanted to continue to be friends with. After all, I didn't have many friends anymore.

That night as I lay in my bed, I thought about my conversations with Charles and how although he was a nice guy, I really didn't know him at all. I started to think about how different my life had become as a single woman. I used to lay in bed at night at the end of the day and share all of my daily experiences with Kyle. Although most of those nights involved me talking until Kyle fell asleep, it was still a cherished memory. But as I lay there, I was alone with no one to share my day with, no one to hold and to feel safe with. I wondered what Kyle was doing at this very moment. I looked at the empty side of my bed and ran my hand across the space that once belonged to him. Just as the bed was half empty, so was my heart.

CHAPTER **12**

A Rainy Season

By the beginning of the week I was eager to return to work if for nothing more than companionship. At work there was so much to keep me busy and since Kyle had never been a part of my job, it seemed easier to forget about him when I was there. But this day would prove to be different. As I sat at my desk managing my morning work, I received a phone call on an outside line. It was Kyle. I was surprised since he had spent most of his time avoiding me, and when I heard his voice my heart actually skipped a beat. Before he even spoke, my mind flooded with ideas of why he was calling. From fearful thoughts that something was wrong with one of the kids, or maybe he needed something from the house, or perhaps, just perhaps this one time, he was calling to tell me that he missed me and really did love me after all. It was none of the above.

"Maddie, I need to talk to you."

And before I could respond, he continued, "I need to know if you have had sex with another man."

I gasped "Why? Why the sudden interest in my sex life?"

He spoke in a condescending tone, "You need to confess your sins."

Suddenly, my desire for him to "love me" turned to anger and I burst into defense mode, with words flowing from me uncontrollably, proof that I was still so emotionally involved with Kyle that I was far from healing.

"How dare you! You don't want me... but you don't want anyone else to have me either! If you think that I will call you up to let you know when and how and whom I have sex with, you are kidding yourself! You are the last person on the face of this earth that I owe any explanation too! I hate you!"

I hung up the phone and tears began to roll down my face. I hated that he could get me to this mental state. I just wanted to get to a point where I could let him say whatever he wanted to say and let it go in one ear and out the other, but I was so far from being able to do that. The door to my office flew open and my supervisor Kay stood there next to my friend Laurel. Apparently my voice was louder than I had thought, and they had come to check on me after over-hearing my conversation. They had both been there for me since my initial separation, and I knew that they were there for moral support and not to chastise me for my loud conversation and slamming the phone on my desk. The look on Laurel's face was sympathetic and she pulled up a chair by my side and placed her hand on my shoulder.

"What happened?"

I couldn't contain myself and I burst into tears. I was not crying because the conversation with Kyle was so hurtful, in reality it was just a stupid comment by him that set me off and I knew that there were many more important things to be upset about. I had cried so many tears that I wasn't sure if there were any left, but today, they came like a waterfall that burst from the mountains during a rainy season. It was just like my life; in a rainy season and I was not sure when or if it would dry up. The emotions would pile up and I would bottle them in until just at the right or wrong moment; a word, a thought, a person, would trigger the emotions and a flood of tears would follow. Laurel had become all too familiar with these moments because she worked with me almost every day. Laurel was a source of comfort to me and she reacted with sympathy and tenderness. Kay was more of an action type of woman. That's probably why she made such a good supervisor. She immediately dialed the front desk and made sure that Kyle's phone calls were not to be put through to me. She gave specific instructions that his calls would be transferred to her and she would let me know if it was important. She was determined to keep me safe from this type of episode while I was at work. The hospital became like my sanctuary from my painful life and she was bound to do everything in her power to keep me sheltered while I was there.

Kay suggested I go and talk to Dr. Wesley and I knew I needed to take a break. I took a deep breath and wiped my tears and I headed down the hall towards Dr. Wesley's office. I didn't want anyone to notice that I'd been crying. I was used to being in control of things and not being able to control my emotions was an embarrassment to me. Kay had called Dr. Wesley to fill him in so he was expecting me. He seemed to know just when to be tough and demanding and when to be soft and comforting. Today he was gentle and his words were soothing. We spent more time discussing how the conversation with Kyle made me feel and how I reacted, and getting in touch with those feelings, than actually talking about what was said. Dr. Wesley was good at putting things into perspective in a way that would cause me to leave his office wondering why I couldn't have figured it out myself. Before I headed back to work, he made a statement I wasn't expecting.

"So I've heard rumors and I've noticed the way Blake has been looking at you."

"Me?" I responded as if to be taken totally by surprise, but actually it was obvious to me and probably everyone else that Blake had noticed me.

Dr. Wesley continued, "I think you should consider noticing him. I think Blake would be good for you."

I wasn't surprised that Dr. Wesley had either heard or seen with his own eyes that Blake had noticed me, but I was very surprised that he had advised me to consider a relationship of any type with anyone at all. But his suggestion was a great distraction to what was going on and it helped to get me through the rest of the day. I couldn't bring myself to talk to Dr. Wesley about my online relationships. The internet chatting thing was so new and few people I knew embraced it. I felt certain that Dr. Wesley would discourage that sort of interaction. I could hear him in my mind telling me that it was isolating behavior, and that I needed to get out and meet real people, and how nothing could come out of these types of relationships. But since I chose not to share this topic with him, I would probably never find out his take on the subject.

    I knew that my relationship with Greg was not something that a normal person would engage in, but I didn't consider myself normal. In fact, everything that I did was experimental and all of the ideals that I had grown up with were being tested each and every day. Greg was becoming a good friend to me and I wanted to meet him some day. If I were to be open and share information about our relationship, then I was bound to open up an avenue for someone to talk me out of it. So for now, I engaged in conversation with Greg almost every night, learning more about his take on life, his feelings towards children, his thoughts on pretty much every subject under the sun, and for now it would remain a secret relationship. I was safe talking to Greg because he was so far away and I was at liberty to share anything I wanted with him, but at the same time able to keep anything I didn't want him to know about secret. While Dr. Wesley was my daytime support system, I had begun to look at Greg as my nighttime support.

    The next day at work I was delivering some paperwork to the opposite end of the hospital before lunch, and on my return, just as I approached the hall leading to Outpatient Physical Therapy, Blake came popping out from around the corner and almost ran right into me. He actually had to put his hands on my arms to keep from knocking me over. I was startled for sure, but there was another feeling in the pit of my stomach that actually resembled butterflies, the kind you get when you are anticipating something exciting. There was a natural connection between us, and as much as I tried to ignore it in the past, it was obvious as he touched my arms that there were sparks that I could not deny.

"Oops, sorry about that!" his face turned red.

Although Blake was very confident and outgoing, sort of the class clown type who loved attention, he seemed to be one of those people that drew his strength in numbers and being alone with another person left him vulnerable.

"It's OK, nothing like a near collision to boost your adrenaline in the morning!"

Blake stammered a bit "Umm... Uhh..." and then managed to get the words out of his mouth as I waited patiently.

"Hey, I'm about to head out to lunch, would you like to come along?"

I accepted almost instantly, "Sure, why not?"

After all, if you think about it, I was following Dr. Wesley's advice, so if nothing else, my lunch with Blake would be therapeutic.

We took my car and drove to a nearby Chinese buffet, and while Blake ranted and raved about how much he loved this place, I kept silent, knowing that they were famous for tempura, which I loathed. We chose a booth by the window and loaded our plates; I picked at the fresh vegetables from the salad bar and peeled the tempura batter off the shrimp and chicken. Blake didn't seem to notice that I was less than satisfied with my meal. He was bubbly and talkative and he spoke to strangers as if they were his best friends. There was nothing awkward about sitting across the table from him. He joked and laughed and had a way of making anyone feel comfortable, no matter the situation. I was impressed to say the least. It was common for men that I knew to be almost intimated when they talked to me. Blake was different, and even though this was the first time I had enjoyed lunch with him, I could tell that he would become a good friend to me. I was sure his fun-loving personality was just what I needed to escape from the dreadful gloom that I had become a prisoner of. I suddenly became aware of why Dr. Wesley thought Blake would be good for me. Through the entire lunch, he didn't ask me one time about my divorce or being a single mom. It was a refreshing change, however, with Kyle and my divorce becoming the topic of so many conversations, I wasn't sure exactly what else there was to talk about. Thankfully, Blake had an unlimited selection of conversation starters, all of them interesting. As I listened to him talk, I noticed that he seemed so happy. His voice seemed to carry a mixture of words and laughter with every sentence. He seemed as though he didn't have a care in the world.

The lunch date was successful and for the rest of the week we had lunch together, either in the hospital cafeteria or some fast food place nearby. I became very comfortable being around Blake and we were becoming friendlier and more personal with each lunch together. Even still, the subject of my divorce and my kids remained elusive. I learned a lot about Blake and we seemed to have a lot in common, primarily, sad ending relationships. Blake had met his estranged wife a little over a year ago. She was young and very religious and lived at home with her parents. According to his story, he slept with her one time and she became pregnant. Her family was very upset and demanded that Blake make an honest woman of her before she gave birth. He said that he felt obligated to her and his unborn child, so he did what he thought was the right thing. Apparently, after the wedding, she refused to move into his house and wanted to continue to live with her parents. This is where his story became almost unbelievable and humorous in a sort of twisted way. According to Blake, she refused to move in with him or have sex with him because, well, he was too large for her and sex with him caused her pain. Of course, I was extremely unsure of whether I was receiving fact or fiction. Having never been intimate with Blake, and having never seen him naked, I could not confirm or deny the truth in his statement.

A RAINY SEASON

He actually made the claim in a very "matter-of-fact" and serious way. I didn't know whether I should laugh, congratulate him on his size, or express my sympathy. Eventually, his wife moved to Arizona with her family and he stayed behind in West Texas. He saw his daughter a couple of times after she was born and continued to send money to her on a monthly basis. His story was sad to me, but it almost seemed as if it worked out for the best for both of them, until you consider that his child would probably grow up not knowing him very well. I asked him if he was getting a divorce and he said she wanted one but neither of them had the money to make it happen.

The next couple of weeks seemed to fly by. Blake kept me entertained at work, and my online relationships kept me busy until 1 a.m. on the weeknights and the kids kept me occupied on my weekends with them. As often as I could, mostly on Saturday afternoons, I continued to work on the painting of the kids. It was coming along nicely and I was sure it would be perfect when I was finished.

It was Saturday evening and I was still not used to having an entire weekend without the responsibility of caring for the kids and for the most part, I felt like I was looking for ways to waste time as I waited for them to return. I opened a bottle of wine and poured it into my favorite long stem wine glass. I grabbed a couple of magazines and cuddled up on the couch for an evening to myself, even though I would have preferred an evening out on the town. At least with no kids at home, I could have a glass of wine without worrying that I'd have too much. I never liked drinking around the kids and it had become my custom to drink an entire bottle on the evenings that they were not with me. Wine seemed to ease the pain of being alone. After my third glass of wine, the doorbell rang. It was late and I wasn't sure who would be ringing my doorbell at this hour. Being alone and slightly intoxicated, I wasn't sure if I should even check, but after the second ring, the curiosity was overwhelming and so I went to the door to look through the peephole. It was Charles. I wasn't sure how he got my address. I'm sure there were a dozen ways that he could have tracked me down, from the phone book, to my home listing, or from conversation in which I was rarely secretive. In either case, I opened the door wide enough to see Charles standing there, but not wide enough to welcome him inside.

"Hi Charles... What are you doing here?

"Sorry to drop by unannounced, but I brought you something."

I didn't see any package or any flowers or anything in his hands. But intrigue coupled with the buzz caused me to open the door wider and step outside on the porch. Charles pulled something out of his pocket that was wrapped in fabric. He started to unwrap the fabric as he began to describe how he had possessed this good luck charm, which was actually a 1938 bronze British penny, for many, many, years. He described how he had taken it to the battlefield during his military deployment overseas and how he believed it had protected him from danger in the past. He said it had traveled all around the world with him and he wanted to give it to me knowing that I was about to embark on a journey of a lifetime with my move to California. It was such a kind gesture and holding the coin in my hands, I tried to decline his offer. After all, if this coin was so precious to him, how could I take it? He insisted and with that, I had no choice but to invite him in to talk.

We sat on the couch and he expressed to me how special he thought I was. My head was spinning a bit and my nose had started to go numb. My nose always went numb when I had too much alcohol and by now you would have thought that I would recognize this as a signal to stop what I was doing and lock myself in a room alone, but I never seemed to heed this physical warning. I did nothing to prevent his advances and a passionate kiss followed. By now, I could feel a flaming desire welling up inside of me. I don't believe the desire was for Charles per se; rather, it was more of a pent-up, sexual energy. I felt compelled to give into my desire, and with my marriage over and my innocence stripped from me, there was nothing that would deprive me of the liberty to do so. However, I realized that in that moment, there was no reasoning, and very little thought if any given regarding the fulfillment of my desire. He was attractive and had a plan and I was very near the border of intoxication, if not already there. Lonely, and with no inhibitions, I fell right into his trap. It was obviously a trap; he carried protection, which was to my benefit because I certainly didn't have my own and unlikely would have been clearheaded enough to use it if I had. I was scantily clad, as I had pretty much retired for the evening with my wine and magazines, and it was effortless for him to unclothe me. I was relaxed and I invited his every touch as his hand gently caressed my shoulder and he slipped his fingers under my strap and slowly slid my top down to my waist. He gently kissed the side of my face and moved down along my neck methodically and tenderly stroking my sensitive skin with the softness of his lips. While he continued to undress me, I closed my eyes and tried to void my mind of any memories that crept up. I was enjoying this experience and the last thing I needed was memories of Kyle cluttering my mind. He was strong and passionate and my body followed his lead as we moved in rhythmic motion to the beat of my pounding heart. But in the end, my heart was just as empty as it had been before. No amount of physical satisfaction could fill the empty space in my heart.

Charles didn't stay long and after the long awaited release in sexual tension and with the effects of the wine, I slept like a baby that night. It only took until morning for my mind to clear, and I began to visit that familiar feeling of deep inner conflict at having just done something that I believed I shouldn't have done. As my sister always says, "Guilt is the most useless emotion there is because once you feel it you've already done the thing you're feeling guilty about." And for me, guilt never seemed to prevent the next time. It only made the perceived wrongdoing easier to repeat since I had already experienced guilt beforehand. I knew

I could deal with this feeling, but I wished I could make sure that no one else knew what had taken place. Since this encounter was so private, I felt that if Charles could just disappear that no one would ever have to know what had taken place. Since I had no way of erasing his existence, I decided that I would contact him and tell him that I couldn't see him again. Somehow, never seeing him again would help me to erase him in my mind.

It was Sunday and the only number I had for him was at his office. I grabbed a phone book and looked him up. I found only one entry with his first and last name and I dialed the number. To my surprise, a woman answered the phone. I thought I must have the wrong number, so I hung up without speaking. Maybe his number wasn't listed and I had reached the wrong person. Still, I tried the number again, carefully pressing the digits on the phone. Once again, I was greeted by a woman's voice.

"Is Charles there?"

"You mean, Charlie?"

"Yes, Is Charlie there?"

I still wasn't convinced I had the right number. He had never given me any indication that he went by the name "Charlie," and he never mentioned any woman, girlfriend, or sister. But how much did I really know about him? Almost nothing. After a minute or two, I heard a muffled voice as if someone had covered the receiver to speak to another person in the room. And then, I heard Charles' voice, or was it Charlie's voice?

"Hello."

"Charles? This is Maddie. I'm sorry about calling you at home, but I only had your office number and I knew you wouldn't be there on Sunday. Who was that woman?"

"Hi there, well, um," he stammered over his words, "I'm going to the office and will be there in about 15 minutes, I'll have to call you from there."

The line then went dead. I sat there for a minute holding the receiver against my ear until the dial tone stopped and a voice came on the line, "If you would like to make a call, please hang up..." I hung up the phone. It took me a minute to think about what had just happened. Was this what I thought it was? Could Charles be married? I was shocked but at the same time, I knew I had been careless. I never asked him if he was married. I don't know why it never occurred to me. I guess I was so consumed with my own problems that I never even thought to ask about his life. The thought that I had ended up in a situation just like that of Kyle's "other woman" make me nauseous. I tried to relax and wait for his phone call. Maybe there was a perfect explanation. Only ten minutes had passed when the phone rang.

"Hello!"

"Maddie, I'm glad you answered."

I didn't have the patience for hellos and how are yous, so I got straight to the point, "Who was the woman who answered the phone?"

"That was my wife."

"WHAT? Your WIFE?" I was shouting by now. I couldn't believe that he was married or that after last night he didn't even try to deny it.

"I'm sorry Maddie, it just happened, you are moving and it just happened."

"How does this just happen? You know what I've been through with Kyle and you know how I feel about Angela and how she should have never let this happen! Now you have put me in the same situation. How could you do this to me?"

"I didn't do it to you Maddie, we were both involved."

I couldn't believe he was making me out to be as guilty as he was. I did not willingly and knowingly sleep with a married man.

"Look Charles, you have to tell your wife, she deserves to know!"

His voice became firm and he sounded agitated. "No! Maddie, this has nothing to do with my wife. You need to keep her out of it."

I was so angry and I felt so horrible that I ended the conversation abruptly. "I never want to speak to you again Charles, NEVER!"

I hung up the phone. I knew that this was exactly what he was hoping for. I would go away, never talk to him again, move to California, and his wife would never learn of his infidelity. For a moment I felt sad for her. But then I thought to myself, "What if Kyle had never told me about Angela? What if he wanted the incident to go away and pretended it had never happened? What if he had continued to be my husband and never told me about the lies?" I would have never known. Our family would have continued to be together, and we'd be raising our children as a couple. And in that moment, I almost felt envious of his wife. She would at least for now be spared the pain that our family had endured. Maybe one day, they would celebrate their 50th anniversary, surrounded by children and grandchildren, no one ever knowing of the night he spent with me. Maybe he would take that night to his grave.

I had always believed that a one-night-stand involved nothing more than a moment of passion shared between two willing partners, with no strings attached. It was on this day that I realized how painful a one-night-stand could be. I knew that this was something I never wanted to experience again. Just the knowledge that there is another person walking around with intimate memories of me and my body was strange enough, and to think that in that instance, that one moment of passion could destroy families and lives made it unthinkable. I decided to let it go. I had to let it go or it would be just another painful experience that would slowly eat away at my already wounded heart. While I knew that I had to take responsibility for my part, I had been a good wife since I was 15 years old and it didn't seem fair that I be held culpable. It seemed that I should be excused for this one moment of carelessness weighed against a lifetime of responsibility. I vowed to myself that I would not let this happen again. For the next couple of weeks, I avoided all contact with Charles, and although I received multiple emails, they went unanswered.

CHAPTER **13**

Parties And Clubs

It was Monday morning and I woke with a severe migraine headache. These types of headaches had become more and more common. My doctor attributed them to the stress I was under. Most of the time, I didn't even think to take over-the-counter medication, I'd just tough it out no matter how bad it became. I guess I had become accustomed to one type of pain or another and having a migraine actually gave me some physical distraction to the emotional pain that I suffered almost daily. In reality, I was becoming more and more aware of what, subconsciously, I had probably known all along; that much of the emotional pain I suffered was from that of my own doing.

I was late to work and even though I'd been a model employee in the past, there seemed to be so many distractions lately and everyone had taken notice of my occasional tardiness. In addition to my children and the normal business of family life, there were the many male distractions in my life. I had also become closer to some of the female nurses and I started to receive invitations to parties and gatherings. Most of the nurses were single or had a boyfriend. There were only two male nurses and they both had a significant other. While I was still happily married to Kyle, I had been unaware of the parties and group outings that the nurses attended after hours. Suddenly, being single seemed to qualify me for this secret world of fun and excitement; however, having children limited my ability to attend most of the time. Interestingly, the nurses suddenly seemed to confide in me regarding relationship issues and men in general. Perhaps being labeled as "married" prevents singles from viewing you as understanding of their issues. It's like there is a clearly defined line and once you cross to the married side, you are banned from the secret conversations of the singletons. It makes perfect sense and seems only natural to confide in other singles when single. The same can be said of married people and secrets. It seems that when you are married, and you want to complain about your husband, you look for another married woman who can sympathize.

Blake ended up working through lunch, so I decided to eat lunch with Laurel in the hospital cafeteria. The food at the rehabilitation hospital was better than most standard hospital food and a lot of the nurses and hospital employees stayed for lunch, so if I felt like being social it was the perfect place to go. The idea of being left alone with my thoughts was less than desirable and the distraction of idle conversation was inviting. Laurel and I chatted about the upcoming going away party for one of the nurses. Lizzy was single and moving to California. The pay for LVNs in California was a lot higher than Texas and every so often we'd lose one or two nurses to the "California Dream." I had arranged a sitter and was actually looking forward to the gathering. Since my breakup with Kyle, I had pretty much lost all touch with our previous mutual friends except for Courtney, who I knew would be there through thick and thin, so being invited to parties with Laurel and the other nurses provided an opportunity for a much needed support system.

Halfway through our lunch, Laurel's best friend Andi joined us. Andi was our age, but with her petite size, her freckle face, and bubbly personality, you'd often forget and think of her as a teenager. Laurel and Andi had devised an entire scheme to surprise Lizzy with a male stripper for the night of her party, but finding one

PARTIES AND CLUBS

in our small town was difficult. For a brief moment, I had a funny thought of how we could ask Blake. At least then it would be easy to tell if he was exaggerating about the reason he gave for his wife leaving him. I kept the thought to myself since my conversation with Blake was in confidence. Eventually, they found a stripper outside of town willing to drive to Lizzy's house for the party. The party was coming up on Friday and we were all excited. Having something to look forward to over the weekend, however, made the rest of the week drag by. I worked hard to make sure my weekends were full when the kids were with Kyle because somehow it made my life seem more normal and a busy schedule helped me get through the weekend without feeling as lonely.

Friday eventually arrived and as excited as I was about going to Lizzy's party, there was a part of me that felt as though I was living someone else's life. All my life with Kyle I had been taught that people who were not the same religion as me were bad association and as the bible says, bad association spoils useful habits. I had been a devout Christian and I had only associated with people who believed in the same religion that I did. I rarely drank alcohol, I never smoked, I didn't gamble, I didn't even watch R-rated movies. But there I was, enjoying the company of women that had many different religious upbringings and frequenting dance clubs, bars, and attending a party with a male stripper. Had I become what my previous religion had warned against? Or was I merely living my life to the fullest? Although I remained confused, I continued on my course, all the while ignoring that little voice in my head that kept trying to squeeze the fun away and replace it with that heavy and monstrous "guilty" feeling. I heard the voice of the religion of my childhood telling me that I was going down a bad road that would lead to disfavor with God and ultimately loss of eternal life, and yet on the other hand I kept hearing the words of Dr. Wesley, who told me that these experiences were necessary for healing. For now, it was easier to believe Dr. Wesley so I would shake the "guilty" feeling out of my head and justify my actions by calling the sinful pleasures I enjoyed "therapy."

Laurel picked me up for the party since she had agreed to be the designated driver. The plan was to go to a local dance club afterwards, and since I never drink and drive, I was grateful for the ride. When we first arrived at Lizzy's house, there were only a few people there. Within a half hour or so, the place was filled with chatty women. A few of the RNs dressed in little nursing dresses, pinafore aprons, and nurse's caps were making their way around the room with a tray in each hand. One was covered with little paper pill-swallowing cups each containing two aspirin; the other with the same pill-swallowing cups, only these were filled with Jello shots. As they moved through the room they would extend the aspirin first and ask, "Would you like to pre-medicate?" Of course, whether you accepted or not, you were offered the Jello shots next. I passed on the pre-medication. I was not a nurse, but from my understanding it wasn't safe to mix alcohol and medication, and knowing how sensitive I was to alcohol, I wasn't taking any chances.

I had to giggle at the concept of nurses offering aspirin with Jello shots. I had always thought of them as people who were careful to follow all the rules, have a healthy diet, and exercise daily. Most of the nurse friends I had acquired lately broke most of the rules at least some of the time, ate junk food as much as anyone else, and exercise meant dancing until 2 a.m. at the local club on the weekends. While I tried the Jello shot, it was too strong for my liking and I waited until no one was looking and dropped it in the trash. It wasn't long before the house was filled with wild and crazy women dancing, singing, laughing, and totally having a good time. I had a few sips of wine, but knowing my own limits, I decided to pace myself at least until we reached the club. Between the music and partying women, it was so loud we almost didn't hear the doorbell ring.

Andi was first to answer the door. About half the women rushed to the door behind her since there had been a lot of talk about what the stripper looked like. Lizzy still had no idea he was going to be there. No one had actually seen him yet and as soon as Andi opened the door, there was a shrill scream of excitement from the houseful of crazed women. Standing there in the doorway was an average-looking man with long, straight hair fully clothed in layers of leather and metal. It was obvious by our behavior that he was in the right place. As he made his way through the front door, he was almost accosted by some of the nurses who had gotten a head start with the Jello shots. He set up his music in the living room while some of the women put him through a 20 questions session and others just stood quietly in the corner, obviously virgins to the stripper experience. I myself, was new to this experience, and honestly even with the bit of wine I had consumed, I wasn't especially impressed with him. Perhaps it was his stocky build or maybe it was his outfit. He almost appeared as though he belonged at a gay man's party. I tried to keep to the back of the room in case the wine made me too honest, because I didn't want to spoil the occasion for everyone else. In a matter of minutes, the music was playing, and without hesitation he started to dance among the brave women who joined him. Then, he attempted to pull in the quite ones in the corner. Andi and Laurel grabbed Lizzy and threw her to the stripper. He ripped his shirt off and pulled her close to him as he moved rhythmically to the music. She was shy and her face turned beet red as she tried to pull away. It only took him about another 10 minutes to strip down to his g-string, and the more he took off, the more repulsive he appeared to me.

As quickly as the excitement began, it had ended. I couldn't help but laugh. I knew at least a handful of men that worked at the hospital with better bodies that would have jumped at the chance to perform for us, but I guess maybe there was excitement in the fact that this stripper was a stranger. I've always felt that a woman's body is much more beautiful than a man's, and in this case, I think it would have been more exciting for me if one of the nurses had done a strip tease. The party was by no means over, but the house was a bit boring after the brief male encounter, and we all decided to go dancing. I was riding with Laurel, so I was in for the duration. I was starting to feel the alcohol and since Laurel was the designated driver, I made her promise to keep me out of trouble at the club.

Several other women and I packed into Laurel's compact car. The music was turned up loud and the car smelled of alcohol. As we made our way to the club, I tried to keep my mind off of my problems, but I realized that it would take a couple more drinks for that to happen. I tried to make sure that it looked like I was totally present, but inside I was still feeling like an outsider. I wasn't sure if my feelings were because of the new experience or because this really just wasn't my scene. In either case, the only way to find out would be to join in and see how I felt tomorrow. It seemed that this was common place for me now; living through experiences only to decide after the fact whether it was an experience worth repeating or one better forgotten.

Once we arrived at the club the drinks were definitely available, as well as a club full of men just waiting for women with problems to show up. I certainly wasn't going to pick up men. I had too many in my life already. But ever since Kyle and I split up, my self-esteem had been low, and any attention from the opposite sex couldn't hurt. The club was musty and smelled heavily of alcohol and cigarette smoke, which usually made me nauseous, but the effects of alcohol made it less annoying. It didn't take long; in fact it was only a matter of minutes before a tall man in his mid 20s approached me. He had the whole cowboy look and the attitude to match. It wasn't usually what I was attracted to, and by the sound of his voice and his demeanor you might have figured that he had read a book on how to talk and act cowboy. While I wasn't particularly impressed and he wasn't especially charming, I was trying to have a good time, and generating attention from this young, somewhat handsome man meant that I wasn't just a used-up mother of three kids after all. So I obliged when he asked me to dance, but not until he bought me a drink. I was already somewhat buzzed, and the extra drink would almost guarantee him a little more fun out of me. I drank the next drink a little too fast, and sure enough, I found myself on the dance floor with "cowboy man" in some type of cross between dirty dancing and full-fledged making out. Time seemed to stand still, and for a moment I felt like I was the only person in the room. Then, I felt a grip on my shoulder yanking me backwards. I turned around and saw Laurel fulfilling her obligation to keep me out of trouble. She dragged me off the dance floor, laughing all the way as cowboy man attempted to grip any part of me and hold on just a little longer to the passing moment.

It's interesting to me how two strangers can share this small moment in time where they engage in a brief, but intimate, interlude which leaves nothing but a small, shallow memory that fades even more with time, and while their paths may never cross again, the very moments that they shared can have a profound effect on their future. Take, for instance, the fact that I had no clue if this man was married or had a girlfriend. Perhaps his friend knows he's married and tells his wife of the moment we shared, which begins an entire process that ends in their divorce. Cynical maybe, but exactly what you'd expect from someone who has seen firsthand how something possibly innocent in the beginning can have such serious consequences.

By the time Laurel dropped me off, I was ready for the weekend to be over and it hadn't even begun. It seemed like the events I scheduled over the weekends without kids typically either weren't quite as exciting as I thought they would be or I would end up making some horrible mistake that I would eventually come to regret. While I kept trying to tell myself the words that I could hear Dr. Wesley saying, "There are no mistakes, merely learning experiences," it was still difficult to avoid the feeling of "regret" for each of the experiences that I wished I had gone without.

I climbed into bed without taking off my clothes or following my nighttime routines. It seemed pointless since I was alone and would wake up the following morning only to repeat the process. As I drifted off to sleep, I wondered what "learning experiences" there were in store for me this weekend.

On Saturday morning, I awoke surprisingly a bit more cheerful than I had been lately. I had plans to spend the afternoon with Blake. This was the first Saturday that Blake and I would hang out. Up until now, we'd been having lunch together and talking on the phone off and on in a very platonic manner. But this morning seemed different as I anticipated our day together. It was obvious that we were physically attracted to each other, yet neither of us had made any type of move to the next level. I knew now from experience that my longing for physical companionship could easily push me to make decisions that may not be the best for someone in such a fragile emotional state, but ever since my separation from Kyle, it would seem that I seldom listened to my own reasoning but instead tended to follow my instincts.

It was nearing 10 o'clock in the morning and Blake would be at my house any minute to pick me up. The date was casual, so I donned my comfortable jeans and a light purple, scoop neck t-shirt. As I grabbed my purse from the dresser, I stopped to reflect on the image in the mirror, and for a moment I almost looked happy. The mirror reflected an outline of a pretty face, the warm rosy glow of my cheeks, the deep blue color of my eyes, and the way my snug cotton t-shirt formed to the shape of my breasts. But the mirror couldn't possibly reflect the pain that, although for the moment remained incognito, was now as much a part of me as the heart that beat in my chest. I was pleased that at least for the day, my face was not suffering the effects from the previous night's tears. I wasn't interested in getting sympathy from Blake. I would rather forget for the day that I had ever been married, and perhaps for just one day I'd feel something normal, though the term normal was difficult for me to grasp having never really ex-

PARTIES AND CLUBS

perienced it. It was at this moment that I realized that I had never really had an opportunity to "date." I had no idea what I was doing. Dating was for kids in high school or college, not for mothers. Yet I was a mother when others were finishing high school, so I excused my self-criticism and finished gathering my things when I heard the doorbell ring.

When I opened the door, although I'd seen Blake many times before, it was immediately apparent why he was so popular among the women. He was tall and handsome and there was something about him that I couldn't put my finger on, but it was something that made me feel safe and comfortable when he was near. His skin was smooth and tan and his body was perfectly built. Blake stood there for a few seconds as my heart flooded with emotions and my body tingled with sensation. My mind raced and I struggled to figure out why I seemed to be holding back my feelings for him. I quickly gathered myself together and greeted him in the same platonic way that I had greeted him so many times before, although I was instinctually aware that a more intimate moment was inevitable. Each time we met, I could sense that Blake's interest in me was more than platonic, and each time my ability to resist became increasingly more difficult. So far our encounters were always in a work environment or during our lunch hour, and knowing myself well, it was only a matter of time before I had a glass of wine with Blake in a more relaxed and non-professional atmosphere and I would no longer be able to resist the temptation.

I stepped out of the house and locked the door behind me. As I turned towards his car, he placed his hand on the small of my back as if to guide me towards it. The air was cool and my sweater was draped over my arm, so I could feel the warmth of his hand through my t-shirt. This was my first time to take a ride in his car. I typically liked having control and ended up taking my own car for our workday lunch outings. He drove a sleek, 1993, midnight blue Firebird. He opened the door for me and as I entered,

I instantly detected the scent of his cologne and the smell of the leather seats. He started the car and proceeded to talk about his car in the way that men often do, the eight cylinders, mean roar, ram air with tune port injection, it's torque, all things that made me chuckle a bit as they meant nothing to me, but you could see his face beaming with pride as he shared the macho car stats and tried to impress me. We headed to a local baseball park where he wanted to introduce me to a group of friends that he used to play baseball with. He explained how important baseball had been to him all of his life and how he would have gone major league after college if he hadn't injured his back. I could hear the pain in his voice and see it in his face as he spoke. It was obvious that sports were important to him, but I think that deeper down he struggled with feelings of failure.

Not being a psychologist, but having spent a lot of time listening to Dr. Wesley, I found myself analyzing his emotional state. From his failed relationship, the distance from his child, his inability to compete in the sport he loved, it all added up. I felt close to him at that moment; we were sort of kindred spirits. I had experienced a deep feeling of failure too. Anything that lasts for 12 years and then abruptly ends can be difficult to adjust to, but when it's a divorce, it feels like your entire life has failed. As I looked across the car at Blake, I carefully examined the tiny lines in his face. He was older than me by at least a few years; I hadn't bothered to ask his age, but it didn't really matter. I thought about how each of us had our own unique experiences that we carried through our lives; how we struggled through difficult times, laughed through happy times, cried through sorrow, and how all of these moments that made up our life seemed to be recorded in the lines of our face.

We arrived at the park, which included a large baseball diamond, a few covered pavilions, and some old wooden bleachers. We mingled with some of his friends and he introduced me as his friend from work. The park was filled with friendly faces, children blowing bubbles, and men playing baseball on the diamond. Everyone that spoke to him seemed to have a similar remark: "We miss you Blake," "Sorry about your back," "You should come out more often." I didn't have the entire background, but it was obvious to me that his being there was bittersweet. We didn't stay long, and although Blake was eager to arrive, he was just as eager to leave. I wasn't sure what he had planned for the rest of the day, but I was happy to just be with him.

We decided to have lunch, but as we drove away from the park he asked if I'd like to see his place. I wasn't sure if there was a hidden agenda or if he really just wanted to show me his place, but I was pretty sure if we ended up alone in his apartment that we would end up taking our relationship to the next level. Although I answered quickly, it seemed that my mind went through a million scenarios in the brief moment between his question and my answer. In that fleeting moment, I had flashes of all the decisions I had made involving men since Kyle left, flashes of Robert in Tennessee, Nick who bought my house, Charles who deceived me, Greg in California, and now there I was again. I wondered what type of image or flash of memory I would have of Blake when I moved to California. I knew that I was not staying in this small town and that it was unlikely that anything long-term would come of my relationship with Blake. I felt so torn between my physical desires and common sense. In my wounded emotional state, I knew that I was hardly competent enough to make sound decisions when it came to sex. I felt so vulnerable, yet so tired of trying to figure out the right thing to do and wondering where I would end up. All I wanted to listen to was the tingle under my skin when I imagined Blake caressing my body. The only other relationship that I was still nurturing was with Greg, and he was a thousand miles away and I'd never even met him in person. I knew I had no obligation to him, although for a minute I felt a twinge of guilt because I knew that I was leading him to believe that I was lonely with no one to keep me company, when in fact there were a number of men available and willing to take over where Kyle left off. Anything that happened there in that moment would be my memory, my past, and I could choose not to share it with anyone in my future. But I was all too aware of how a moment that belongs to me when shared with another person becomes their moment as well and could easily come back to haunt me.

It was a short drive to Blake's apartment complex, and as we drove up in front of his unit, I felt that he could sense the same build up of instinctual, almost animal-like anticipation of what was to come. As he killed the car engine you could almost hear the beating of our hearts. Neither of us reached for the door handle right away as we sat for a moment in the car as if to consider the consequences of the event that we both knew was about to unfold. And then Blake broke the silence.

"Here we are!"

"I see. So tell me what is so special about your apartment?"

He paused for a minute, put his hand on his chin, and wrinkled his face, as if to come up with some extraordinary feature that would set his apartment apart from the other approximately 200 units in his complex that were bound to be similar if not exactly like his.

"Well, I have a great large screen TV."

"That is the contents of your apartment, I asked what makes your apartment special?"

He grinned, "Well, lets go in and I'll see if I can answer your question."

So we both hurried out of the car and headed to his front door. I got there first, and as he came up from behind me, he put his left hand on my waist as he reached around me on the other side to open the door. As the door opened, his left hand was still on my waist, and it felt as though he gently guided me past the entrance and into a short hallway that led to his modest one-bedroom apartment. We were almost instantly in his living room, which connected to his dining and kitchen area. His furniture and decor seemed typical of a bachelor, with the exception of a large, luxurious couch centered directly in front of a large screen TV. This was definitely a bachelor pad and Blake seemed to pay extra attention to the comfort level surrounding the TV, which was a clear indication of how he spent much of his time off work. The dining room furniture was absent and in its place rested a weight bench in the middle of what looked like a total body workout center. His kitchen was small and sparsely decorated with a lone toaster on the counter. I could see his entire apartment from the living room except for the bedroom and bathroom, which were behind a closed door that led off of the living room. Blake was still behind me with his hand on my waist and as I stood there, unsure of my next move, he came around and stopped right in front of me. He was so tall that when he was that close, I had to look almost straight up to see his eyes. I leaned my head back and as our eyes met I felt a tremendous amount of heat sweep through my body. He looked into my eyes and slipped both of his arms around my waist to pull me even closer. I didn't resist. He leaned forward and, to my surprise, he began to sing to me in a very deep and sexy voice. It was my favorite song.

And without further hesitation, he gently brushed the hair away from my neck, leaned down, carefully placed his lips on the curve between my neck and shoulder, and kissed me gently. He continued to gently open and close his lips as he kissed me ever so slightly, moving his way up my neck to my ear. As he pulled my earlobe between his lips, I bit my bottom lip and closed my eyes. His lips were sweet and he seemed to have practiced this move to perfection as if it were an art. He brushed his lips along the side of my face as he worked his way to my mouth. His lips were moist and soft and they parted as he took my bottom lip into his mouth very gently, in a playful way, as he pressed his hands against my lower back, forcing my hips towards his body. I literally felt like I was going to melt. I think this moment was the first time in my life that I had ever felt true ecstasy. With just this kiss, my body quivered and I never wanted it to end. The tender tug of my lip turned almost instantly into a deep and passionate kiss. His hands moved from my waistline to my hips and he lifted my body against his so that my toes actually left the floor for a moment as we embraced. Still locked in this embrace, he lowered me to the floor again as he guided me backwards towards his bedroom door. He never took his lips off of mine as he backed me against his closed door and reached to turn the knob behind me. The force of our bodies against the closed door propelled us towards the bed as the door swung open. The bed was soft and it was obvious that he paid attention to comfort in the bedroom just as he did with the sofa in front of his big screen TV. As he lay atop me, the down comforter came up on each side of my body as I sunk into his soft mattress. I felt as though I was floating on a cloud as he slid his hand beneath me and reached to unfasten my bra. My heart pounded and the anticipation was becoming overwhelming. His hand slid around to the front of my body as he cupped my breast in his hand. He continued to kiss me, and when I opened my eyes, I could see that his eyes were open. He looked at me intently each time his lips met mine. His hands carefully slid along the sides of my body as he raised my arms and slipped my shirt and bra off easily over my head. I reached for his t-shirt and slid it up the side of his body, and as he tugged it over his head, I could feel the warmth of his chest against my breasts. We slithered out of the remainder of our clothing and I could see his biceps flexing as he used his arms to keep his weight from coming down too hard on my naked body. I felt as if he was holding back, perhaps afraid from his past experiences that I couldn't handle his massiveness, so I put my arms around him and pulled him into me as he rose and fell over and over again. As we reached climax together, I could no longer harness the intense pleasure and I screamed in ecstasy.

The entire encounter lasted maybe 15 minutes, but it was one of the most sexually fulfilling 15 minutes of my life. Something about Blake was so intense, and even immediately after our connection, he left me longing for the next time. There was something very animalistic, something primal about this experience. As I lay nearly breathless next to him, naked and glistening with his sweat, he ran his fingers along the curves of my body, which sent chill bumps up my arms. I had experienced true ecstasy. It was with Blake that I sensed a turning point in my life. I believed again that there was something more for me than Kyle, something that I had not experienced that was available for the taking and that I truly deserved.

CHAPTER **14**

Temporary Satisfaction

Blake and I spent the entire weekend together, either in his living room watching movies on his big screen TV or in his bedroom, where I discovered a passion for sex that I never knew I had. Blake knew exactly what he was doing, and although I had been married since I was 15 and had sex countless times with Kyle, nothing had ever compared to the pleasure I experienced with Blake. He was gentle, yet wild, and he introduced me to a whole new experience of sexual pleasure.

I only checked on the kids a couple of times over the weekend. Kyle was probably happy about that since he accused me of trying to infringe on his time with the kids when I would check up on them during his visitations anyway. I completely abandoned my online connections. At least with the internet, when you don't log in, it's like the people you know there disappear. It's easy to ignore them when you want to, but you end up having to explain your absence when you sign back in. I didn't care because I was completely caught up in Blake. Although we had become close friends up to this point, now that we had become intimate, there was something that seemed even stronger than our friendship. It was the chemistry, the passion between us, and the unspoken language when we touched that bonded us. Although it was nice to be friends and we had great conversation, the relationship had changed, and the sexual intimacy seemed to be the most important aspect.

Although our individual circumstances were different, they seemed similar enough that without even saying it, there was an understanding that this relationship would end. I knew his goal was to move closer to his daughter and he knew I was moving to California. We had talked about Greg, and Blake knew that I was considering meeting him in person. Blake was extremely easy going and non-judgmental. It wasn't that he didn't care, he just wanted to make every moment that we spent together something special. I wondered if it was possible for me to fall in love with him. It was clear to me that I was nothing more than infatuated, and whether it would or could be possible to become true love didn't matter since I had already set my mind to the fact that we were temporary. I had never imagined myself in a temporary relationship, especially one that felt almost entirely physical. I had always imagined that being the sort of thing that men did. In a sense, we were both using each other as an outlet for the pain we'd been suffering in silence. It was like the intense desire that we shared together marked the beginning of the end of a dark cloud of loneliness. Whether it was Blake or someone else in my future, I recognized that I could and would eventually feel something for someone else and that the pain of losing Kyle would someday be replaced with a deeper and more intense feeling for someone else.

Sunday night, I sat in front of my computer chatting with strangers and others whom I called "friends" about things we had in common, complaints about society, and our dreams and ambitions. I didn't see Greg online until just before I was ready to sign off. A chat window popped on my screen.

"Hey you! Where have you been?"

Greg had noticed my absence and surely attributed it to my healing and getting on with my life. In a sense he was right, although I left out the part about how that also entailed spending much of my time with Blake. Although I was having fun with Blake and he was a true friend to me, I saw Greg more as my future. He was where I was going to be and he seemed to be the stability that I needed in my life. He talked about his two little girls, his sister, his mother, his job and how he couldn't wait to meet me. Up until now, the reality of meeting Greg seemed very distant. I wasn't a believer that this type of relationship could work after my first attempt didn't turn out so good. Although I still kept in touch with Robert, I often wished I had just remained a long distance friend and not become intimate with him. Of course with each intimate relationship, I felt some sense of regret. The regret was not necessarily related to the act itself, but just the knowledge that someone out there had experienced a very private part of me was haunting. I hated becoming someone else's sexual history. There was a time when I was proud that I had only been with one man and that I was the only woman he had ever been with. But now things were different. I knew I could never regain that innocence, and although I was in control of who I slept with, I knew that unless I found someone that I could trust again, someone to love forever, that there would be more regret to come.

It seemed almost impossible that I would ever love anyone the way I loved Kyle. My love for Kyle was unique. I grew up with him and once believed that we were meant to be together. I remember lying by his side and holding him and telling him to promise that he would always love me. Although he promised, it was all too clear that in the moment you experience love, you say things and make promises that you believe at the time that you will keep, but on the other side of tomorrow no one really knows what is to come. The thought of a marriage that lasts a lifetime seemed so unlikely now, and part of me figured I would end up in a loveless marriage of convenience. After all, if marriage wasn't going to last forever, then at the very least it should be beneficial for the short term whether financially or sexually. From my chat with Greg, I believed that he was financially well off and he was intellectually stimulating.

BEYOND THE PRESENT

Almost daily, Greg talked to me about my plans to move to California and asked me if I had found a job. I'd been looking and found a temp agency that was willing to hire me and guaranteed me that they would be able to find me a job. The pay rate was double that of what I received in Texas. The agency was in Citrus Heights, California, not far from Sacramento. My move was getting close and I had already taken care of most of my business by phone, like paying the deposit on my apartment complex, setting up my bank account, and contacting the temp agency. But Greg was persistent and he really wanted me to fly out ahead of time to meet him. He suggested we meet in Los Angeles. Greg would pick me up at the airport and we would drive to Laguna Beach and spend the weekend together. I was tempted by the fact that Laguna Beach was a gorgeous seaside resort and artist community and how it supposedly had the most beautiful beach in southern California. It was late and I was lonely again and the thought of visiting a beautiful beach sounded so good to me. Before I signed off that night, I consented.

For the next several weeks, I spent every free moment with Blake, although I was still nurturing my online relationship. Blake satisfied my physical needs, but there was something about Greg that seemed to meet my hunger for intellectual connection. I had always been a deep thinker. I loved to analyze things and calculate all the "what-ifs." No conversation was too controversial for me. Although growing up in my religion, the most exciting topics were not allowed and I had learned to keep most of my opinions and feelings to myself. Even sharing them with Kyle could become dangerous. In our religion, the man was to be the head of the household and he was to preside over his family. If I introduced what was considered "independent thinking," he would most certainly suggest that I meet with the Elders of the congregation. It seemed to be his answer to everything, even in our own intimate matters. While our religion was not as strict as many religions that teach that the only purpose for sex is for procreation, even among married couples, many sexual acts were considered abnormal or deviant. Masturbation, all premarital sex, and all non-coital forms of marital intercourse were strictly prohibited. If we ever were tempted to engage in any oral sex, Kyle would quickly feel remorse and often suggest we talk to the Elders in the congregation to help us overcome our temptations. I was absolutely against talking to anyone about our sexual relationship and always believed that if it felt right and we were married that it was okay. Now that I had experienced Blake, I was introduced to a whole new world of pleasure. Between the physical pleasure with Blake and the intellectual satisfaction that I found in conversations with Greg, it seemed my needs were met. But deep down, I realized that I had totally lost my religion. I actually found myself doubting the very possibility of the existence of a God in heaven.

I wondered if my doubting that there was a God was real or if it was some psychological way to help me to continue the life of sin that I currently led. Every moment that I spent with Blake, no matter how much pleasure that I gained from our relationship, was laden with guilt. Yet I continued to meet him and to stretch every boundary to its limit. It was like when I was with him my body became possessed with some rebellious teenage girl with raging, out-of-control hormones. I was physically unable to resist him and driven to seduce him every chance I got. Perhaps never having experienced being a real teenager led me to this careless behavior. I justified each sexual encounter with the fact that I had been with only one man for 12 years of my life and a responsible mother since I was 17, and I blamed my young marriage and religious upbringing for depriving me of gaining sexual experience. I rebelled at every possible opportunity, like the time I climbed on top of him with my body wedged between him and the steering wheel and we had sex while he was driving down the road, or the time at his apartment where we opened the dining room drapes as wide as they would go and turned on all the lights after dark and had passionate sex on the weight bench right in front of the window. One weekend, after I had returned home from spending the day with him, I heard a knock at my bedroom window. I was scared at first, but then I heard Blake's voice. I opened the window and let him in and we spent the entire night making love. Our relationship had become almost purely sexual. During the workweek, I went to work and I did my job, although we flirted and touched each other every chance we got. We agreed not to share the details of our relationship with our mutual friends, although I told Laurel and I was sure that he had told some of his friends by the way they looked at me in the halls.

In the evenings I spent time with the kids, playing with Barbie dolls with Katy and Kaliegh and helping Levi read instructions for his video games. After they went to bed, I escaped to my alternate reality of online relationships I had built with strangers. On my weekends with the kids, I painted, I helped them with homework, and I cooked and played with them as if we were still a perfectly normal family. And on weekends without them, I had wild and crazy adventures with Blake.

I managed to have little contact with Kyle. Every conversation with him led to arguments and angry words being exchanged. He wanted to know what I was up to. I wasn't sure if he was jealous or just so used to controlling me that he had a hard time letting go. There was a time just before our divorce was final that Kyle actually asked if I thought we could get back together for the sake of the kids. I asked him what I felt was the most important question, "Do you love me?" His response was "No, but I think I could learn to." I knew that I deserved better than that and I was convinced that he knew that I would decline and merely asked the question to hurt me even more. But now I had control again. Whether I was making irrational decisions or not, I was finally in complete control of my life. Unless you consider the fact that the perceived control was in fact a lack of control since I would give in to every whim and desire that came over me. But it didn't matter, just as long as Kyle was not in control.

TEMPORARY SATISFACTION

It was the night before my trip to California, and Kaliegh and Katy were with Kyle for the summer. Kyle moved to California ahead of me and was staying with his parents until he could get a job at a fire department. I was letting my mom spend as much time with Levi as possible before we moved, which was a big help for me as well since I was busy packing and of course planning my trip. I spent the night at Blake's house and as we lay in his bed, we talked about what would happen in California and how I would feel when I returned. Although Blake insisted that he had been exclusive with me, I had never asked him to be, and I had no time to be with anyone else even though he would have been okay with me doing so. The basis of our relationship was pleasure, not love, and in the absence of love there seemed to be an absence of jealousy. Even so, I explained to Blake that if I ended up having sex with Greg, that upon my return we could no longer be together. No matter what my conscious allowed me to do, I knew that I could not be with two men at the same time. Blake understood and didn't try to change my mind. I was moving only a couple of weeks after I returned from meeting Greg, and if it turned out that Greg and I were intimate, the last weeks working with Blake would be difficult for both of us. But all along, I knew that our relationship was temporary. It was driven by a need to rebel, a need to be wanted and to unleash physical desires. Deep down, I knew this was our last night together, and as I lay across his chest and he ran his fingers through my hair, I could sense that he feared the same.

The next morning, I left early to go home and pack for my afternoon flight. I only confided in Blake and Laurel that I would be going to California to meet Greg. Everyone else assumed that I was going to go out to California to get things settled before my move, and I left it at that. Blake drove me to the airport and we said our goodbyes and as he pulled me close to hug me my skin tingled and I already missed what we had shared together for the last few months.

BEYOND THE PRESENT

My flight felt all too familiar, going to meet a stranger for the second time in six months. This time it felt safer since I had spoken to Greg's sister and his children on the phone. He seemed more like a real person than Robert had. I felt like I already knew him, since we had been communicating for longer than I had been with Blake. When I finally arrived, it was just as I had expected, and thanks to pictures that we had exchanged, I recognized him right away. I could see the excitement in his face as I approached him. I wasn't nervous, but at the same time, I didn't feel excited. Our first embrace felt as though I was meeting an old friend. Perhaps the chemistry between Blake and I had made it nearly impossible for Greg to compare. He was very polite and his personality matched exactly that of his letters. It is hard to explain, but I was used to hearing his voice on the phone and reading his letters, and now to see his lips move and the sound of a familiar voice come out of this unfamiliar body seemed strange. Greg was not as attractive as Blake, but his personality made up for it. Even so, I was used to our conversations without being in his presence, and I almost wanted to close my eyes as he spoke. For a moment, I thought how wonderful it would be if I could combine Blake and Greg into one man and how that together, they would make a perfect lifelong partner. We had an hour to talk in the car as we made our way to Laguna Beach. There was hardly a moment of silence, and even though this was the first meeting in person, it was easy to talk and we picked up right where we left off in our letters and phone conversations.

We arrived in Laguna Beach and I was surprised to be staying directly on the water. Greg had made reservations at an inn on the top of a seaside bluff just a few steps from the local village. The views were spectacular and the shops and restaurants were all within walking distance. I only brought one carry-on bag since the trip was only for a weekend. We took our bags to the room and decided to go down to the shops for a bite to eat. As we walked, we talked about all kinds of things, and just as I had already discovered through our online conversation, we had much in common. Just before we were to cross the street, Greg reached down and held my hand. And once again, it was obvious that while I cared for Greg as a friend, there just wasn't the same kind of spark that I got when I was near Blake. While I had never considered myself a superstitious person, I always tried to listen to my gut instinct and even absent the sexual desire for Greg, for some reason something inside told me I was on the right path. I recognized that lately I had not been listening to my gut, but instead giving into passion and rebellion. I knew that my move to California was already in motion and even though I was moving to an apartment, I would be close to Greg, and I felt the need to continue to nurture the relationship. It was for this reason that I not only consented, but also made the first move that night in the hotel room. Greg would have been perfectly content to just sleep next to me in the bed that night, but I felt like I had to know if there was anything there between us. And not surprisingly, once again, what would otherwise be great sex paled in comparison to my experience with Blake.

The weekend was enjoyable; walking along the beach, eating delicious food, great conversation, and in a short time it was time to leave and go back to the life that I was so eager to run away from. I knew that now things would be different between Blake and me. While Blake knew all about Greg, Greg knew very little about Blake. I just couldn't bring myself to lie to Blake about my being with Greg. And even though it wouldn't stop Blake from sleeping with me again, I just couldn't carry on two sexual relationships. It was the one "forbidden" thing left intact in my conscience.

CHAPTER 15

A Symbol

It was the morning of the Fourth of July. I had a 4-day weekend and I was avoiding Blake because I knew it would be difficult to resist his advances. I was feeling antsy. I felt that this Fourth of July needed to mark some significance in my life. I tried to think of something I could do to symbolize my own individual freedom; the freedom to make choices in my life, choices for myself no matter how frivolous they may seem to others. First, I thought about a tattoo. I never really considered myself a tattoo person and I had no idea what image I would choose to symbolize how much I had been through. I decided to take a trip to a tattoo parlor to see what my options were. I had to drive to a neighboring city to find a parlor in the first place, and being the Fourth of July, I was surprised when I found one open. The place was small and appeared to have been converted from a small single family home to a business. The building was old, but not run down. On the door hung a sign that read "OPEN" in large red lettering. As I approached the entrance, there were a few old cowbells that were tied to strips of leather, and as I opened the door they clanked together and a dull, tonal sound resonated.

I heard a man yell from a back room, "I'll be right with you... Have a seat."

I looked around the empty room, which had a few chairs

placed along the wall each with its own unique style, and they appeared as though they were handed down a few generations or picked up at a local estate sale. I picked the chair that looked the most stable and sat down on the soft cushioned seat. The walls were thin and I could hear the sound of the motor in the tattoo machine in the next room.

Once again, the cowbells clattered as a young man and woman who appeared to be in their early twenties entered, and once again I heard the man yell from a back room, "I'll be right with you... Have a seat."

The couple sat across the room from me and after a moment of silence, the woman asked me if I was getting a tattoo.

"I'm not really sure, I just want to find out what my options are."

"Well I have five tattoos and now I'm getting my belly button pierced."

She showed me some of her tattoos, a butterfly on her ankle, a cross on her upper arm, a flower on her neck. She described the reasons behind her choices and told me about how painful it was to get the one on her ankle. She had about 10 earrings in each ear and a large, silver ear cuff. She was excited to be getting her belly button pierced. I hadn't really thought about piercing as an option so far. I already had my ears pierced, three on one side and one on the other. Anything more than ear piercing seemed way over the top to me at the time and the thought of a naval piercing scared me, but a tattoo sounded even scarier and even more permanent. I wasn't sure what I would do until the man came out of the back room covered in tattoos over most of his upper body. Right behind him, another man came out and they shook hands and the heavily tattooed man left the building. Then the man who I presumed to be the owner asked who was next.

"I am."

"Well how can I help you miss?"

A SYMBOL

"Well, I was thinking about a tattoo, but I'm thinking I'll get my belly button pierced instead."

I looked towards the young woman whom I'd been conversing with and she smiled and said, "Cool."

The man brought me back to the room he had just come from. There was a cushioned reclining table that resembled what you see in a doctor's office. There was a nearby table scattered with sterile gauze and several objects that I couldn't identify. I figured they must have been tools of the trade. He asked me to sit on the cushioned reclining table and asked if I'd ever had a body piercing. I explained that I'd only had my ears done when I was 16. He proceeded to give me some information about potential risks involved. He said it so matter of fact, almost as if he were reading it. He had me sign some papers and then showed me a selection of jewelry to choose from. I made my choice, a black titanium naval ring. He explained to me how it was the best choice because titanium is a biocompatible metal and is used for surgical implants and is lightweight, and durable. He asked me to lie back on the table. I lay back and took a deep breath. He asked me to lift my shirt and expose my belly button. I did so and he sized up my midriff and proceeded to mark little dots on my belly with a felt tip marker. He then swabbed my naval area with some type of antiseptic and reached for a surgical type clamp. As he pinched the skin around my naval, he clamped it onto me to stabilize the tissue for the puncture. This step was extremely painful. The clamp was so tight that the skin seemed to get cold and numb. He pulled out a very long, very sharp, hollow needle and, without warning, very carefully forced it through the clamped tissue where his dots were marked. He placed the jewelry on the end of the spear and guided it through my piercing. The pain was intense but brief, and although I made no noise, my eyes filled with water and I bit my bottom lip so hard it almost bled and that was it, it was done. After giving me a few instructions on how to care for it, he processed my payment and I was on my way.

BEYOND THE PRESENT

I had to drive home with my shirt pulled up and my pants unbuttoned. The stinging sensation continued throughout the day. I thought about how displeased my father would be if he found out what I had done. He was against any type of body piercing, even ears. I decided I didn't have to tell him. In fact, if I didn't want to, I didn't have to tell anyone. This made me feel even better about my decision. It was like a silent symbol on my body that replaced the scarlet letter "D" that I had been wearing and would serve as a constant reminder of the decision that I had made, that no matter what, I would never depend on a man like I depended on Kyle. If I were to ever fall in love again, I'd be sure that the man I chose was an enhancement to my life, not a necessity.

The following morning the throbbing sensation and stinging pain of my new piercing was quickly forgotten as the realization of how close I was to my move began to set it. I knew I needed to make arrangements for a U-haul to take my things to California. I thumbed through the phone book until I found a rental location not far from where I lived. I picked up the phone to make the call. A man answered with a very deep voice.

"I need to see about renting a U-haul to take to California in a couple of weeks."

"We have them available."

"Can you tell me what the price would be for a one way trip?"

"You aren't coming back?" He sounded almost disappointed, as if in the last two sentences I had spoken to him he had already become fond of me.

"No I'm not, I'm moving. Do you have any discounts? Because I am a single mom and I'm not made of money."

I think at this point it was the single mom comment or maybe it was just my tone, but the sound of his voice turned less professional. He seemed to speak with a smile on his face and I tried to visualize what he might look like.

"Weeeeellll..." he drew out the word as if to evoke anticipation from me and then he continued, "If you come in to the shop and fill out the paperwork to reserve the U-haul and are wearing short shorts, I might give you a discount!"

At first I was shocked and appalled by his unprofessionalism, but that only lasted an instant when I considered that I stood to save a lot of money by just wearing my everyday attire into the shop to fill out the paperwork. My second thought was how in the world did he know I would even look decent in short shorts? Maybe he figured I would surely decline if I were overweight or hideous. Or maybe it didn't really matter and he liked the sight of all women in short shorts, big or small. In either case, I thought it was quite odd and figured he must not get out much or see women often, or perhaps he did this all the time and there was some thrill in inviting scantily clad women to the shop so he could check out their legs. In the end, it seemed harmless to me so I played his game and convinced him that my legs were extra special and I made sure to get the regular price and agree upon a 50% discount while we were on the phone.

I decided that I would go there immediately to make sure and secure my discount since this guy might not even be around in a day or two. There was no need to change in to short shorts since I was already wearing them. It was, after all, West Texas in the heat of the summer. I got in the car and drove to the U-haul rental shop, which was only a few miles from my house. I felt kind of strange when I pulled up and thought for a minute, what if this guy was just messing with me and had no authority to give me a discount? Perhaps he was just going to get a kick out of watching me walk in and embarrassingly ask for my discount for wearing short shorts. I decided to approach it a little differently and ask for him by name.

"Is Steve here?" I asked as I approached the counter.

The tall slender man turned around and yelled over his shoulder. "STEVE!! You have a customer!"

Out from a back room came a young man in his early twenties, about six feet tall, with large shoulders and a strong muscular build. The instant he saw me you could tell by the smile on his face that he was sure that I was the one he spoke to on the phone. I glanced at his tag and noticed the label under the nametag, "Manager." At this point, I was pretty confident I'd actually get my discount. I didn't like the demeaning way in which I had been dealt with, but the discount was significant, and since I was leaving this town behind me, it didn't make sense to go to his superiors or make a case out of something that was clearly going to end with me saving money, walking away, and never seeing this person again. So instead, I played along. In fact, I figured I had the upper hand. He wasn't controlling me; I was clearly controlling him. I was a customer that he found attractive and all I had to do was be my friendly self and he would reduce the standard price of the rental. It seemed fair enough to me. I smiled and turned around in a circle as if to model my short shorts and my lean, tan legs. He gave a few oohs and ahhs and muttered some statement as to how the discount was totally worth getting me to come into his shop. I gave a half fake laugh and asked him to put his money where his mouth was. He pulled out a contract to reserve the largest U-Haul they had one way to California for half the advertised rate. I took the signed copy and didn't waste any time leaving. He quickly came around the counter and followed me out to my car. All the while I was walking away from him, I could hear him insisting that we go on a date before I leave. I wasn't about to date him and the very fact that he made advances on the phone before he met me and was now following me to my car kind of gave me the creeps. As I opened my door and got inside my car, he jumped between the car door and the car so that I couldn't close the door. He squatted down beside my car as I put my seatbelt on and started my car. This surely was enough for him to see I wanted to leave and wasn't interested in his date proposal. As I reached for my car door I told him thank you and explained that I had to go. He held the door tight so that I couldn't close it. My radio was on and the music filled my car with lyrics about leaving and the desire to stay. Steve immediately picked up on it and swore to me that it was a sign.

"It is totally not a sign!" I exclaimed. "I am moving to California and some guy at a U-Haul rental place who gave me a discount for showing my legs is not going to change my mind."

He seemed to get a little aggressive and I decided it would be best to just be nice and leave him with a possibility that I might contact him. He was twice my size and I didn't want any type of physical confrontation to take place. Especially because the parking lot was behind his shop, which was not on a main road and there was no one else around at the time. I went from firm to soft and agreed that maybe it was a sign. I asked him to write his number down for me and he quickly went from aggressive to docile. As he released the door, he reached in and tried to place his hand on my leg. I grabbed his hand and explained in a joking way that I barely met him and we'd need to at least go out on a date or two before he could touch my legs. He laughed a little and let me close my door. I rolled my window down a bit and told him I'd be sure to call him. I drove off with no intentions what-so-ever to call him and quickly lost his number. As I drove away, I realized that he had my physical address and my phone number and that I would need to be extra cautious for the next week and a half. Then I'd be off to California and none of this would even matter.

For the next few days, Steve called me and left messages on my machine a couple times a day. The calls always went unreturned and on some of the messages he would indicate that he was sure that I was avoiding him. At least he had that part figured out. I knew that he would be there the day I picked up the U-Haul and that I would have to face him. I decided it would be best to arrange for my younger brother to go along with me when I picked it up, just in case.

By now, most of my family had shunned me for not returning to the church. Out of five brothers and five sisters, I felt as though

I had lost all but one sister, who had already left the church before me, and two younger brothers, who had left as well. My brothers had left the church some time ago and they had been in and out of trouble ever since, and one of them was actually serving time in jail. I had two half-sisters that were older than me that I rarely contacted, mostly because of our age difference. I knew one of them had left the church after a divorce, but I wasn't sure of the religious status of the other. When I called my youngest brother, Brandon, to see if he would help me pick up the U-Haul, the conversation turned to the possibility of him coming to California with me. It seemed like such a great idea! He would babysit my kids while I worked in exchange for room and board and some extra spending money. With the California income that I was to receive, it fit well within my budget and it would be nice to have a helper on the 1600-mile drive across the country, especially since I'd have Levi with me. He wanted to get away and felt the experience would do him good. He was five years younger than me and was still trying to figure out what he was going to do with his life. Before the conversation ended, it was a deal. He would move with me to California, and at any time that he changed his mind, I agreed to buy him a ticket to fly back home.

My friends at work had planned a going away party for me. I was excited, but also felt sad because I knew that my move was designed as an opportunity for me to leave behind the life that I lived while married to Kyle. I knew that these friends had only been in my life for a short time compared to the number of years I'd been in Texas, and I knew it would be difficult to keep in touch with them once I started my new life in California. For the last week and a half before my move, I kept busy packing and avoiding Blake because I knew that it would be difficult to resist his advances. I had stopped communicating with most of my online friends, with the exception of occasional chats and emails from Robert and of course, keeping in touch with Greg. But now it was Friday night, and I would be seeing Blake as well as saying my final goodbyes, since I would be off to California with my brother Brandon and my little Levi. I sat down on the edge of the bed before getting ready to go, and as I looked around my bedroom, my mind was flooded with memories of Kyle and me in that very room on that same bed, exchanging stories from our experiences during the day, making plans for vacation, talking about our children, and making love. My life had changed so much in the last seven months, and now it was about to change even more. In fact, I felt that my life was not really changing, but that I was about to start a brand new life surrounded by new people, new experiences, and making new memories. Even my name had changed. I imagined it must be similar for someone involved in a witness relocation program. For a minute, as I sat on the bed, I felt the need to hide. My whole life seemed very surreal. I quickly got a hold of myself and decided that I wouldn't think so deeply. Everything was happening now and there was no turning back. I slipped a lightweight tank over my shoulders and stepped into my frayed denim shorts. The shorts rode low on my hips since my naval piercing was still tender, and I felt that tonight would be a fun time to reveal it, although some of my nurse friends already knew about it. I was surprised to find out how many of them had already pierced their own. In fact they had actually pierced each other's with a 12-gauge hypodermic needle, and they teased me for paying for mine.

    The party was at Andi's house, and although I arrived on time, the party had already begun. There was loud music, dancing, drinking, and loud conversation. I barely made it in the door before hands started grabbing at my belly button. I had to guard it carefully to prevent all the germs on the grasping hands from causing an infection, not to mention that the entire area was very sore. I made my way to the kitchen where I filled my glass with Dr. Pepper when no one was looking. I wasn't drinking because I was driving that night, and I had a long drive ahead of me the next day. It almost didn't seem right to be sober at my own going away party, but I knew my limitations when it came to alcohol, and I wasn't about to put myself or anyone else in danger. I had come this far and I was eager to see the rest of my life unfold. It was easy to make my friends think I was drinking. Most of them were drunk already, so all I had to do was laugh and hold the glass in my hand and everyone assumed I had rum and coke. All my friends were hugging me and telling me they were going to miss me. I wondered if that were the case or if they were just really happy to have a reason to celebrate.

As I headed around the corner through the dining room and into the living room, I caught a glimpse of Blake in a far corner. I protected my belly button as I walked through the crowded makeshift dance floor to Blake. As I approached him, I could almost feel the temperature of the room rise and all I could hear was the beating of my heart. When I reached him, he was leaning on the arm of a couch. He reached his arms out and placed his hands on my hips, as he looked me over from head to toe, stopping when he saw my belly ring.

"Nice," he said, and I proceeded to tell him how a tattoo was my first choice and gave him all the symbolic reasons that I chose the ring instead.

He pulled my body close to his and he placed his lips on the side of my face and whispered in my ear, "How you holdin up?"

The scent of his cologne combined with his warm breath on my ear made me weak at the knees. He knew exactly how I was holding up, he knew that it was extremely difficult for me to avoid him, and he knew how bad I wanted him. At that moment, I wanted to grab his hand, run out the door, and take him to my house to make wild and passionate love just one more night before I would be gone and probably never see him again. But it was my party and everyone was there to visit with me. I knew that it was not only the party that was keeping me from escaping with him. There was a sense of satisfaction to know that I could be strong against his temptation, but I wasn't totally sure why I was fighting it. It wasn't the guilt of having sex outside of marriage; I had accepted the fact that I would not remain celibate, but on the contrary, had every intention of exploring my sexuality before ever choosing to marry again. It wasn't my commitment to Greg, as I had no idea if I would ever become serious with him in the future. It was more likely the fact that being with Blake again may have actually made me want to stay, and I knew that Blake was not the marrying type. I couldn't live in this town anymore and I couldn't let anything stop me from leaving, even the most pleasurable experience of my life. And so I resisted Blake and I knew that it was hard for him too. He pretended to be okay with it and we danced, talked, laughed, and mingled until the party started to die down. I had to go home and get some sleep before my trip, and so after saying all of my goodbyes, Blake walked me to my car. Before I got inside, he placed his hands on both sides of my head and guided my lips to his and delivered the most passionate goodbye kiss I could have ever imagined. I wanted to melt in his arms. Blake looked as though he was choking back tears and the emotion he showed caught me off guard since he had always seemed so unattached. At that moment, I thought about how maybe, in another life, another time, perhaps we were meant to be together, but it was too late. I had chosen the direction I would go and I was sticking to my plan. After one last hug, I got in my car and headed home. Driving away, my body still tingled from his touch. I honestly doubted that I would ever have that much chemistry with any other man.

CHAPTER 16

Moving To California

It was Saturday morning and Brandon, Levi, and I were packed and ready to go. I had successfully fended off Steve at the U-Haul store, avoided another intimate moment with Blake, and said my goodbyes to the people who mattered. It was time for me to take off across the country in a 24' U-haul that towed my Honda Accord. My future awaited me 1600 miles away. We left early and traveled as far as we could every day, stopping at the first sign of sleepiness. I was incredibly careful on the road. It had only been six years since I lost my little sister, her husband, and their unborn baby in a car accident after my brother-in-law had fallen asleep at the wheel.

It was April 18, 1990 when I last spoke to my little sister. Tommy and Ann had been living in Colorado and worked in California over the winter months. Spring had arrived and they were headed back to the mountains in Colorado where Tommy was living the life of a real cowboy, herding cattle, breaking horses, and mending fences. But to Ann's surprise, Tommy was changing the plans. He had called when I was visiting at my mother's house and told me that he had decided that he was going to head straight for Texas. Ann was eight months pregnant with their first child and he was sure she'd be sleeping, so he planned to drive all night long so that when she awoke in the morning, she would be delighted to find out that she was going to see her family instead of returning to Colorado. He made me promise not to tell her the plan before he called her to the phone. I talked to Ann about her pregnancy and she described to me how much her baby kicked, how awesome the feeling was, and how excited she was that she was only a month away from holding her newborn baby. I told her I loved her and reminded her to wear her seatbelt on the long trip home. The next day, April 19, 1990, as I was wrapping the tiny baby clothes and little baby blanket that I had carefully hand crocheted as a gift for Ann, I heard a knock at the door. I expected that it was my Mom letting me know that my sister had arrived, since I was living next door at the time. I opened the door and found my sister-in-law with a dreadful look on her face.

She bluntly blurted out, "There has been an accident and Tommy and Ann and the baby are dead."

Kaliegh and Katy were only two-and-a-half and five at the time and were playing on the living room floor. I immediately burst into tears and hysterically screamed, "NO! NO!" as I swung at her and called her a liar. I couldn't believe something so tragic had happened to our family. That moment had forever changed me, causing me to become a more paranoid mother with an overprotective tendency towards my children. It also made me a more careful driver. I saw how hard their deaths were on our family, especially my mom and dad.

Brandon and I drove for 34 hours and I was so happy he had decided to come. Driving alone with a three-year-old would have been incredibly difficult. The scenery on the way to California was beautiful and was a pleasant change from the West Texas desert view. I arrived the night before my apartment was ready, so Greg opened his house to us. It was almost midnight when we arrived in Citrus Heights, California. Brandon pulled out a small flashlight and read the printed directions to the house while I drove. Levi was sleeping soundly strapped in the middle seatbelt with his head resting on a pillow that was wedged between him and Brandon.

MOVING TO CALIFORNIA

It was almost 1 a.m. when we approached Greg's house. We had stopped to call him only two hours earlier so he knew when to expect us. His porch light was on and we pulled up and parked on the street in front of his house. It was too dark to really see the house, but Greg had already sent pictures of the modest, ranch-style home with a neatly manicured lawn, and of the pool and hot tub located in the back yard. I grabbed a small bag, Levi's pillow, and my purse, and Brandon picked up Levi and laid his head on his shoulder. The trip was long and Levi was exhausted. Before we made it to the front door, Greg had already opened it and came out to meet us. He grabbed the bag from me, leaned over and gave me a kiss, and then led us into the house. We made a bed on the floor for Levi next to the couch where Brandon would sleep. We were so excited about finally arriving that we couldn't sleep, so Brandon, Greg, and I stayed up for a few more hours talking about the move, the apartment we would be staying at, and our plans for the next week. Eventually, we realized that Levi would be waking us up in a few hours hungry and ready to start his day. I tucked the covers around him as he lay peacefully on the floor next to Brandon and made my way to Greg's bedroom. By the time I saw the bed, I realized how tired I was and I slipped off my jeans and crawled in the bed. Greg went to get a glass of water and I was asleep before he returned.

The next morning, I stayed in bed as long as Levi would let me. When I woke, Greg was sleeping next to me and I could hear Brandon and Levi in the living room. Although it was Monday morning, I didn't have to start my new job through the temporary agency for another week. Greg was teaching classes at the local University in the afternoons a few days a week, so he was available to help me move into my new apartment, unpack, and get familiar with the area. I looked around the room and tried to soak up as much as I could of these unfamiliar surroundings. I took special mental notes of the pictures around the room. There were pictures of his little girls and they looked very happy. There were a few statues on the dresser of some oriental origin, and since Greg was half Japanese they seemed appropriate. He seemed to have a lot of knick-knacks and the room was a bit cluttered for my taste. I looked over at Greg as he was sleeping and suddenly realized that I was in a stranger's bed. Of course, I knew him as much as you can get to know someone by email and chat, but I didn't really know him. I started to feel almost like a lost item. I was lost in the same way that when you lose a pencil at the park and someone finds it, they keep it for a while and then because it's not theirs, they don't take great care of it and it gets tossed somewhere for someone else to find. Obviously, my life was of more value than a lost pencil, but I realized that, most importantly, I needed to find myself.

That afternoon, Greg, Brandon, and I moved my belongings from the U-Haul to the apartment. The apartment was a small two-bedroom with one bath and a very small kitchen with an even smaller eating area. Katy and Kaliegh would share a bedroom when they came back, Brandon and Levi would camp out in the living room, and I would take the master. The master, however, was smaller than the kid's room in my previous house. It was cramped, but it was all that I could afford on a single income. Child support was an issue, because although the court had ordered it while I was living in Texas, it didn't help quite as much now with the higher cost of living in California. I knew that once Kyle had a job, I would have to request more support to compensate. It seemed that Kyle's biggest issue with paying child support was that he was giving it to me. He had no problem buying things for the kids; he just didn't want me to control the money. Kyle didn't seem to realize that the support paid is to cover his portion of the extra expenses that are generated by having children, such as electricity, groceries, water and sewer, having a larger car to transport them which takes more gas, school lunches, and daycare to name a few. I'm sure in Kyle's mind, he figured that I had free daycare, but even though Brandon was my daycare for the

MOVING TO CALIFORNIA

time being, I paid him and provided room and board as well as food. But to Kyle, because he was giving me a check, it was like he thought he was supporting me and not the kids.

The apartment was sufficient for the time being. Fortunately, I had found a temporary job at the U.S. Fish and Wildlife Service and I started the job before the girls returned from visitation with Kyle. I worked with an all male group and the job was less than rewarding. I spent most of my days doing word processing, typing letters, filing, and answering phones for a group of approximately 12 geologists. On one occasion, I got to take a field trip with one of the Geologists to a Fish Hatchery. This proved to be the most exciting part of my job. It became apparent to me that my job there would never become permanent. There had been significant layoffs and there were previous government employees who were on waiting lists to be rehired. I decided that I needed to keep my eyes open for a more stable job if I wanted to be able to afford the California lifestyle. Late one evening after Brandon and Levi had gone to sleep, I lay across my bed on my stomach looking through the classified ads for a new job. I came across an ad for "Fund Information Specialist" for a local investment company. The ad read, "Respond to telephone inquiries about our products, market conditions, fund performance, and policies and procedures. Requires Bachelor's degree or equivalent experience, one-year prior sales experience or marketing, and a NASD series 6 license (must be obtained within 90 days) with training provided for eligible candidates. Knowledge of financial industry sales or service experience is a plus."

I had no financial background, no degree, and I had no idea what a NASD series 6 license was, but something stood out. I circled the words "with training provided" and drew three large stars beside the ad. There was one thing I was still confident in and that was my ability to learn. I knew that if I could just get a chance to have an interview that I could convince them that I was the person to hire. Learning had always come easy to me and all

I needed to do was read a book to learn a new skill. Surely if they were training for this job I'd stand a chance.

Greg and I dated and it was just like I had imagined that real dating worked. Since I didn't have any real experience with dating, I didn't really know if there were rules to go by, so I made them up as I went along. I looked at my time spent on chat with Greg as dating, so even though I slept with him the first time we met in Los Angeles, I didn't consider that our first date. Greg was a communicator, which was a breath of fresh air for me. We spent a lot of time talking about things, deeper things. Kyle and I had conversations, but they tended to be on the lighter side. We would discuss what the neighbors were doing or our friends' parenting styles, and maybe where we would like to go on vacation. My conversations with Greg were more philosophical in nature. We discussed books, meanings behind actions and attitudes, and human nature. We also talked a lot about our kids. One thing that was for sure was his undying love for his two little girls. This was one thing we both had in common, and yet sometimes it was the fuel for arguments. As much as we had in common when it came to conversational style, we didn't always see eye to eye on the best parenting style.

As soon as I could I told Greg all about the job opportunity at the investment firm. He was very excited for me and since he'd worked in the field in the past, he had a lot of good insight as to what the job would entail. I called the number in the ad and was informed that there was to be an interview process at a hotel lobby all week long. The hotel was on my way home from work and I decided that I would stop by on Friday to see if someone could see me. Greg did his best to prepare me for the interview and filled me in on all kinds of information relating to stocks and bonds and market conditions. It was more than I wanted to absorb at the time, and I wasn't too concerned for the time being since the ad indicated that they would provide training. So as well intended as his lectures were, I tried not to think too much about what the job would be like and what kinds of duties I'd be performing.

MOVING TO CALIFORNIA

When Friday arrived, I was sure that everyone at my temporary job was aware something was going on when I showed up wearing my best suit, especially when the dress code was business casual Monday through Thursday and casual on Friday. I wasn't trying to keep it a secret because everyone knew that my job at the Fish and Wildlife Service was temporary, but still no one asked me why I was dressed up. I had a hard time thinking about work that day. My mind kept wandering and I tried to visualize what the upcoming job opportunity might lead to. My life didn't feel settled yet and I knew that deep down, my desire to find a new job or meet new people was only a temporary distraction from the fact that I was still not over Kyle. How could I get over a 12-year marriage in merely seven months? However, I knew that no matter what I wanted or how badly I missed the relationship that Kyle and I once had, that there was never going to be a chance to go back. So many things had changed. My life would never be the same. All of my views, whether religious or political, my family values, my level of innocence, had all changed. I was not the same person that Kyle left, and that was a scary feeling. Honestly, I wasn't sure who I was. Outside I was still Maddie, a daughter, a sister, a mother of three children, but it was time to rediscover my inner self. It was time to decide what I did in my spare time, what hobbies I enjoyed, what things were important to me, and what I liked, or more importantly, didn't like in the opposite sex.

It was finally time to leave and I hurried with anticipation to the hotel where the interviews were being held. As I stepped into the lobby, I saw rows and rows of chairs that had been placed in a large open area and a small desk sitting towards the entrance to the room. A nicely dressed woman greeted me as I approached the desk and asked me if I was there for an interview.

"Yes I am!"

"Please sign in on this sheet and have a seat and we'll call you when it's your turn."

"Oh, ok, well, uh, how long is the wait?"

"It will probably be an hour. As you can see we have a full house today." She turned and nodded towards the room full of interviewees seated in the lobby. This was not what I expected at all.

"I really don't think I can wait for an hour. I was thinking I would be seen right away, so I think I will have to pass, but thank you anyway."

I turned to make my way towards the entrance, but before I turned completely around she stopped me.

"Wait! Let me see if someone can see you now, I'd hate for you to leave." She stood up and opened a closed door behind her and stepped inside.

I looked around the room and realized that people were staring at me. I'm sure that they wouldn't be happy if I were to bypass the line and get interviewed on the spot. I wasn't the one to make that decision, so I smiled and then looked away as I waited for her return. The room was very quiet except for the sounds of rustling papers as people reviewed their resumes and the sound of people clearing their throats or shuffling in their seats. The door where the receptionist entered was cracked and it made the voices inside the room accessible. I couldn't make out everything that was said, but something to the affect that I was well dressed and that I might be a good candidate. I was still slightly uncomfortable about the prospect of cutting in line and I wished that she would hurry back, if for nothing else than to send me on my way so I would no longer feel the stares from the impatient people waiting to have their chance to interview. She finally returned after what was probably actually only a minute or two at the most but seemed like a very long time.

"I have someone who can interview you now!"

I was totally surprised, but also a bit embarrassed. There were a lot of people waiting and I was sure that at least the people in the front row of seats who could hear our conversation were probably not happy that I was being interviewed ahead of them.

But before I had much time to worry, a gentleman stepped from the back room and extended his arm to shake my hand. He took me back to a large room where there were many tables like the ones you see in a school lunchroom. At each table there was an interviewer and an interviewee. It was noisy enough that the sound drowned out the voices of the people so you couldn't hear exactly what was being said between them. I'd never been interviewed in this type of a setting before, but was happy to have the chance. I had always been good at communication, and answering the questions that he asked me came easy. I wasn't sure if it was because I was suited for the job or if I just knew what things he wanted to hear. Much of the questions related to customer service and I prided myself in my ability to handle difficult situations with people. It seemed ironic to me that I was skilled at making people like me, but at the same time, somehow, my husband of 12 years managed to stop loving me.

My interview went well, and while the man who interviewed me was very professional, there was that feeling that I was getting preferential treatment. I was never sure if it was because I was blond or because I was thin or if it was my smile or maybe it was all in my mind. I was confident in my abilities, but interviewing always left me wondering if it were my skills or my looks that put me in the running for the job. It didn't really matter, I mean who in their right mind would turn down an opportunity if they found out they were hired strictly for their looks? It has been said that a good interviewer leaves you wondering if you will get the job or not, but I left feeling sure that I would get a call the following day with a start date.

Even though I was confident in my customer service skills, I was being interviewed for a position in which I would need to understand all things "investment." I had never paid any attention to investments in my life since there was never any money to invest anyway. I had no idea about stocks, bonds, options, futures, and market conditions. It was like a foreign language. And when the interviewer shook my hand and assured me that I would hear something very soon, I felt butterflies in my stomach. I'm sure in part because I was excited about a new opportunity, but there was a part of me that asked myself afterwards, Can I even do this?

Two days passed before I got the phone call offering me a job, and without hesitation I accepted. My hours were to be 6 a.m. to 2:30 p.m. It was a perfect job for me; Brandon would be there to see the kids off to school and I would be home when they returned. The excitement about the new job was overwhelming. I was informed that I'd be paid for six weeks of training and at the end of that period I'd be required to take a test to pass my Series 6 license. I wasn't sure at the time what that meant, but I was confident that I could pass anything I put my mind to. So I spent the next six weeks learning during my work hours, studying at night, reading nothing other than the Wall Street Journal, and basically fully submerging myself in the investment world. My kids had returned from their time with Kyle and my life became very difficult. Between studying and managing the kids, I had little time to spend with Greg, and when we were together, we spent most of that time studying for my test. We had become very good friends and it seemed natural to be lovers as well. But even still, I had pushed my feelings aside for the time being and refused to take a look at our relationship too closely. I didn't have time to worry about love and somehow, for the time being, I managed to suppress the pain that I was suffering.

On some days I felt like I'd be studying forever before I understood all the concepts. But all in all, the six weeks of studying went by very fast, and the test date finally arrived. The were about 15 of us testing, mostly men. It seemed that the financial industry was primarily male, unlike the nursing industry where I was accustomed to working. I was sure that the men had an advantage on this test because I'd always believed in the myth that women were superior in verbal ability while men excelled in mathematics. As we entered the room, I tried not to think of who had the advantage or whether I knew more than the others or even enough to pass. The one thing I was sure of was that this was it! I had already learned as much as I could in six weeks and this was the place where I would find out if I was cut out to do the job. It was a pass/fail test. I had to get above a 70%.

The Series 6 exam, which sounds much less intimidating than its official name, "The Investment Company/Variable Contracts Products Limited Representative Qualification Examination," consisted of 100 questions on topics such as securities markets, investment securities, economic factors, tax regulations, prospecting and sales, and more.

I knew that I had 135 minutes to complete the exam and that I could spend no more than 1 minute and 21 seconds on each question. I knew that 23% of the exam would be over the most difficult sections, which included securities markets, investment securities, and economic factors. I had studied, and although I felt sick to my stomach, I was as ready as I would ever be. I had to budget my time and flag difficult questions to go back and answer after answering all the simple questions. We were guided to our seats, which were small desks with a computer monitor and very high walls that separated each station. On the desk was a notepad to be used as scratch paper, two pencils, and a calculator. I was very happy to see the calculator. I looked at the screen and I knew that when I clicked 'begin test,' that the following 135 minutes would determine my future path. I carefully read each question all the way through before I answered. When I wasn't sure of the answer, I used tactics that I had learned that would help me guess more accurately, like using the process of elimination to narrow down the probable answer. I tried to take deep breaths and not rush and I used every last second of the allotted time to complete the test.

It was finally over. I'd taken the test and had done the best job I could do. Fortunately, we received our test results quickly. I had passed the test with a 76. It was a pass/fail test, and even though my first thought was that I'd made a "C," I was quickly reminded of the fact that on a pass/fail test a 70% is an A and a 71% or above is an A+. I was happy to have passed, but even happier that I would not be let go from my job. The hours were perfect and the money was great too. I needed this job to continue to live in California. The last thing I wanted to do was have to move back to Texas because I couldn't afford to be on my own in California, and I was determined to make my new life a success.

That evening was celebration time. Greg and I went out to dinner and made plans to celebrate even more by going to Reno over the weekend. Brandon kept the kids while we were away. I needed this little getaway to think about my life and where I was headed. But thinking about my life was not what happened that weekend. Instead, I got caught up in the moment, and on a whim I ended up getting married in a small walk-in wedding chapel in downtown Reno on October 26th.

When we returned, my brother and kids were as shocked about my marriage as I was. I can't say exactly why I did what I did, perhaps I felt that by remarrying so soon, I was somehow validating my worth, or perhaps I wanted Kyle to see how easy it was to replace him. Whatever the psychological reason behind it, I should have known better. I moved in with Greg right away, and while the first few months of our marriage went by quickly and without incident, partly because of being so busy changing schools for the kids, packing and unpacking, and working non-stop, it was only a matter of time before it became obvious that our friendship was not enough to sustain a marriage.

I had married Greg only a little over six months after my divorce with Kyle was finalized. Even though I thought I knew him and he thought he knew me, it became very clear that we were different people. I don't think that either of us tried to lie about who we were. I think it takes time to get to know all the little details about the inner person. Our already doomed relationship was riddled with strife from the beginning. I ended up accidentally getting pregnant, only to miscarry a few weeks into it. The pregnancy was unexpected, but once I lost the baby, there was the guilt of feeling that it happened because I didn't want to be pregnant. Greg's life was a financial mess and I ended up caught in the middle of that as well. Kyle had remarried and moved to Washington State, and we had constant arguments about the kids and child support, and those arguments filtered over into my relationship with Greg. I remember the time when Kyle brought his new wife with him to pick the kids up for his visitation. I had never met her before, and I was eager to meet the person that would be tucking my children into bed at night while they were so far away. When he arrived she wasn't with him.

I met him at the door... "Where is your wife?"

"I dropped her off at the convenience store before I came here."

"Why?" I was shocked and Kyle just stood there with a satisfied look on his face.

"Because she doesn't want to meet you."

That was the final straw! I lost it. I refused to give him the kids unless he brought her with him to pick them up. My babies were flying to another state and while Kyle worked as a firefighter for 24 hours at a time, this woman would be spending time with them, feeding them, caring for them, and taking my place as their temporary mother. How could she not want to meet me? I knew that she had children of her own and I wondered what type of woman wouldn't understand another mother's feelings on this subject. Was Kyle doing this to stir things up? Was he doing this to make me angry? Did she really not want to meet me? Whatever the reason behind his decision, I was extremely upset. Rather than calling the police to force the custody issue, Kyle left and talked her into coming back to the house to meet me so I'd hand the kids over to him. At this point, it would have been difficult to actually look her in the eye and feel comfortable about her being the one to care for my kids in my absence, but I hoped for a miracle. When he returned and I opened the door, I remember the blond woman standing there with her arms crossed, her sunglasses still on, and a not so happy look on her face, and I remember her words.

"I'm not sure why you need to meet me, it's not like we are going to be friends or anything."

It was then that I realized that it would have been better not to meet her at all. At least not knowing who she was or what type of person she was I would have been able to imagine a nice face being sweet and loving to my children, taking them for ice cream, reading to them, and tucking them in bed at night. At this point, I was sure to have nothing but thoughts of this hateful person who stood at my door. For her to have this attitude towards me, it had to come from Kyle. Whatever he had told her had soured her towards me and there was nothing I could do to change her mind, just as this very meeting would set the tone for my future relationship with her. It makes perfect sense if you think about it. How can a man who cheats on his wife start a new life without making his ex look horrible? Who would want to be with a man who admitted that he cheated on his previous wife and fell out of love with her after she gave birth to his 3rd child? It had to be easier for him to make me look like the bad guy and gain her sympathy in the process.

It was bad enough that Kyle and I couldn't work things out and be civil while parenting our kids. With the emotional and physical distress of my miscarriage coupled with his financial burdens, the fighting between Greg and I became extremely intense and I found myself crying more than laughing. I don't even remember what the fights were about. Most of them were probably trivial. Some of them were about rules for the kids or Levi's dirty hands touching his clean suit coat. But there is one fight that I remember very clearly, and it was the one fight that made me realize I couldn't live that way any longer. I remember yelling and screaming and trying to get away from the emotion and the pain. I ran through the house into the back yard, and fully clothed in the middle of the night, I jumped over the hot tub and into the swimming pool. It was a perfect place to cool off. Although it seems almost funny looking back, at the time it was a pivotal moment. Not the fact that I leapt over the hot tub, or the fact that I could have broken a leg if I had not cleared the hot tub, but it was the words that I remember Greg saying to me when he came outside afterwards. I figured he had come outside to make up or to bring me a towel or to apologize for something.

He stood across the other side of the pool and I remember him saying, "It's always all about Maddie, isn't it?"

The words were painful to hear. If it was all about me, then why was I still with him when I knew deep down that I wasn't truly in love with him? After all, I had talked myself out of leaving him once before. It was a month or so before this fight when I had visited a nearby apartment complex on my way home from work. I actually left a deposit check to hold the apartment, only to return the following day to take it back. I knew I didn't love him, but I couldn't hurt him they way Kyle had hurt me. For some reason, I thought I could stay in the relationship and that love wasn't important. I'd heard of relationships where married people stayed together for the sake of their children or for financial reasons, but now it was all too clear to me that marriage without love would never work for me and wasn't fair to him.

Perhaps he was right. Maybe it was all about me. Maybe I wasn't staying in the relationship to keep from hurting him. Maybe I was in the relationship because it was easier than accepting the fact that I had made a bad decision. It was easier to stay than to admit I screwed up. My relationship with Greg was not about love it was about dependency. Not the type of dependency you would imagine. I wasn't dependent on him financially, and he surely wasn't meeting my emotional needs. I merely needed to be needed. I needed someone to want me and to depend on me. But now he had made it easier for me. With those few words, "It's all about Maddie," I could now accept them and instead of staying for him, I could leave for me.

◄ BEYOND THE PRESENT

So there I was, less than a year after getting married for the second time, facing the reality that it was time to move on. I had no idea which direction to go. All I knew was that whichever the direction, it would be without Greg.

CHAPTER 17

A New Job

Even though I had decided that this relationship would not last forever, I wasn't ready to end it. I needed to save my money and have a plan first. All too often, I made hasty decisions that I ended up regretting. I wanted to be sure that this relationship could not last before I severed it. There were many lives that would be affected by my decision to leave. So I waited and planned, but deep down I knew that I just needed time to adjust to what I knew was inevitable.

The kids were away and I was finding it more and more difficult to concentrate on my job, and I quickly grew tired of the commute. It was Saturday afternoon when a neighbor stopped by to ask if Greg was looking for a job. There was a job opening at a local Fortune 500 technology company. It was the place that everyone wanted to work, but it was very hard to get a foot in the door. Greg had already taken a job somewhere else, so I decided to look into it. It wasn't a job that I had ever done before, but now that I had been hired working with stocks and bonds, my self-confidence had risen and I felt sure that I could do anything I set my mind to. It was a long shot, but I submitted my application anyway.

Within a week, I had an interview. I was excited about the new opportunity. My brief marriage was falling apart and it felt like a new job would be opening the door to a brand new life. I had opened so many doors already, and with each door I entered, I seemed to exit wondering why I was even there in the first place. My choices were simple, give up or keep going. I had never been a quitter, and if losing my husband after 12 years and moving over a thousand miles away to start a new life only to find myself in another failing marriage didn't do me in, then I was sure that I could get through almost anything. Some people tend to crumble under pressure, but it seemed to almost be a source of motivation for me. Sometimes, I would get so excited and so motivated about things that there was a part of me that just felt like I was in this body for the ride, and I wondered where it would take me next. This time was no exception. I showed up the day of my interview braced for anything, or so I thought.

When I walked in the door to the office building, a young woman who appeared to be in her early twenties greeted me. She had light brown hair and seemed almost over-dressed for the casual office. She looked me up and down quickly as if she was trying to read me by the way I was dressed. I always dressed professionally for interviews. It didn't matter what type of job I would be doing, what mattered was the realization that I only had one chance to make a good impression. The job I was to be interviewed for was a technical position, but after sizing me up, she immediately asked me if I was there for the secretarial position. I wasn't surprised and I didn't take it as an insult. It was a technical position and I was sure that more men had applied than women since that seemed to be the trend with the growing technology industry.

I answered politely, "No, I'm here for the LAN Technician interview."

She escorted me to a room and asked me to sit at a large table and explained that there would be a gentleman that would come in and give me an assessment test in a few moments. Those few words were enough to drown every bit of confidence that I had managed to muster up over the last few days in preparation for the interview. I sat there terrified of taking the assessment test for a couple of reasons. First, I knew this interview was for a position that I had no experience with, and second, I just hated tests. This was one type of pressure that I knew I didn't thrive under. After about 10 minutes, a short, stocky man entered the room. He was wearing glasses that made him look very smart. He had a couple of sheets of paper in his hand and a pen. I stood as he entered the room and we shook hands as he introduced himself as the company technical specialist and sat across the table from me. He explained that the questionnaire that he had in his hand was comprised of technical questions, including questions about local area networks, TCP/IP, and various other acronyms that I was completely unfamiliar with. I interrupted before he could finish with his description of the test.

"I'm sorry, but I need to explain that I don't have the technical expertise that is required to complete your test. If you are looking for someone with those particular skills, then I am not the one for the job, however, if you are looking for someone who is a fast learner, dedicated, and enthusiastic, then I am the person you are looking for."

I was fully expecting that at this point I would be thanked and escorted out of the building. But he persisted.

"Well, I would like you to just take the test so I can see how much you actually know about networking and then we can go from there."

I was not going to give in. I refused to document that I knew nothing about networking and had none of the skills that were required to perform the job.

"I can tell you that I don't know anything about networking. And if I were to complete your test, it would only have my name on it."

He had a look on his face that was a cross between rejection and disbelief, but it quickly turned to a sad look as if I had just told a little boy that I would not play his game. I waited for his response as he sat there looking at his test. Finally, he popped up out of the chair and told me he'd be right back. A few minutes later the woman who greeted me when I arrived showed up and once again escorted me down the hall to another room where she asked me to be seated. I looked around the room and wondered why I was still there. Surely they had better candidates who didn't refuse to take the assessment test.

A few minutes passed and I was greeted by two women; this time, a blonde and a redhead both about my age. They were very outgoing and personable. They didn't seem to be bothered or even mention that I had not taken the assessment test. They both had a copy of my resume and we chatted about my previous skills and my interest in art and graphic design, and then they described the position. The position description once again sounded very foreign to me. There was talk of hubs and switches and network diagrams, all of which I had no experience with. I was just as adamant with them as I had been with the previous interviewer that I had none of this technical experience, but that I was willing to learn and excited about the opportunity. Aside from my lack of experience in networking, both women seemed to like me. They seemed to take special interest in my graphic design abilities. But just as every good interviewer should do, they left me hanging, not knowing if I would get the job or not.

There were so many reasons that I wanted this job; the pay was better, and the new experience would be great for my resume. But there was something else. It seemed like I was becoming accustomed to change. While my once steady routine of being a wife and mother was all I really needed in my life, it was now as if the rush of adrenaline that came with each new life change had become a welcome trend in my life.

Only about two weeks passed before I received the call with the news that I had been selected for the position. I was both excited and terrified. I was asked to come in and fill out some

A NEW JOB

paperwork and was told that my new boss wanted to meet with me. There was no hesitation on my part. I was growing tired of the stress of working with fluctuating markets and unhappy customers. Working in the Fund Information Department, people rarely if at all called you to tell you they were happy. For the most part, there were calls from angry fund owners wanting to know what the fund manager did with their money and demanding I have a crystal ball to tell them if they should pull out or stay in. Needless to say, I promptly turned in my notice with my boss at the financial institution that I worked at. I don't think she was surprised because there was a high rate of turnover in the industry, especially in her department.

I made an appointment with my new boss and when the time came, no matter how confident I had been in the past, I was now extremely nervous. My boss' name was Bryan Rates. While the women I had met on my first interview made me feel extremely comfortable, the same could not be said for this encounter. I wasn't sure whether to call him Mr. Rates or Bryan, but he quickly broke the ice and asked me to call him Bryan. He shook my hand and asked me to have a seat. The job was in actuality a contract position. I would be an employee of Valateka contracting to the larger technology company. After explaining the general duties and expectations of the job, Bryan took me by surprise with his next comment.

"I want you to know that it took a lot of convincing for me to agree to hire you. Not because of your lack of experience in the field, but because I think you are too pretty to work with the group we have onsite and I anticipate it causing problems."

I was shocked, but I shouldn't have been. I was no stranger to this type of sexist attitude. But on the positive side, he did agree to hire me despite his feelings. I wasn't totally sure what type of problems he anticipated, but could only speculate that he worried about sexual harassment. It was hard to believe that in this day and age that grown men would have problems maintaining a professional attitude at work towards women, no matter how pretty the woman. I was used to working with all men and I assured him that I could handle it and appreciated his agreeing to hire me. I recognized that it would have been very easy to not hire me and blame it on a number of things, from my lack of experience to my refusal to take the technology test. It was for this reason that I was not offended, but it did make me wonder what type of men I'd be working with that made him worry so much.

The job wasn't to start for a few weeks, and I took advantage of the time and purchased all the networking books I could afford. I had already learned so much in such a short time when it came to the financial industry, and I knew that I could do the same with networking. The last thing I wanted to do was to show up as the new "Network Support" hire and have no clue about networking. I figured that if I was working with almost all men that they would respect me a little more if I had some knowledge of the industry. But even with all the studying, I was still nervous about that first day of work.

I showed up willing and ready, but there was so much to learn that it was almost overwhelming. Lisa was one of the women who interviewed me and she was primarily responsible for convincing Bryan to hire me. She was a few years younger than I, but she had her degree and was highly skilled. She was invaluable when it came to helping me learn the ins and outs of the job requirements, but also in filling me in with the social surroundings.

We were located in a temporary building that was attached to the main site building. It was actually one of several large metal trailers and had been nicknamed T2. The trailer was packed with cubicles, with one long center isle leading to the main entrance of the main site building. My spot was in a cube on the end of a row of cubicles right next to the aisle so that everyone who entered or exited the building through the main site would walk right past me. There were so many people and so much to learn about the culture, not only within the larger company, but also within the smaller contracting company where I was employed.

A NEW JOB

One of the first things that I learned was the badge system. The contractors, like myself, wore orange badges and the actual company employees wore blue badges. It didn't take long to realize that there was a clear social status distinction between the blue and the orange badges, at least for most of the people. And it was clear from the beginning that most of the orange badges had the ultimate goal of becoming blue badges. As it turned out, Lisa herself was being offered a promotion and would soon be wearing a blue badge, and I was hired to take her place. On my first day of work, there was a large sign that hung on the outside wall of a nearby cubicle displaying the words "Congratulations Austin" in big bold letters. Lisa filled me in on the details, and apparently Austin was formerly a contractor with Valateka and his first day as a blue badge was my first day as an orange badge. You could tell the Valateka employees really liked Austin and were happy to see him get the blue badge status. It seemed that the blue badge people who had formerly been contractors were a lot more down to earth and were less likely to look down on those they left behind. I had a lot to learn both technically and socially, and the whole experience was exciting, but also emotionally draining. I have always been a very outgoing person, but this time I felt like there was a lot of pressure on me. First, I knew that I would be scrutinized since I got this job with little or no qualifications, and second, I knew that I was being watched closely since my new boss already anticipated issues with my new fellow employees.

One of the first people that Lisa introduced me to was Tom Green. Tom had only been hired a month or two before me, so we had at least that much in common. We were both sort of rookies. Tom was also very outgoing and always joking around. It didn't take long for the two of us to click. It felt almost like a brother/sister relationship, which was unusual for me. I was used to the type of guy that only wanted to really get to be friends with me if he had a possibility of getting something else in the long, or short term for that matter. Even though Tom was a big flirt, I didn't take him serious because he had recently begun dating someone, and he knew I was married, even if unhappily so. I wondered if it was really possible for a man to just be friends with a woman with no interest in sex. However, I was pretty convinced at this point in my life that even those types would sleep with me if I offered. For a while, it almost felt like my relationship with Tom was that of a mutual case study of the opposite sex. We were both pretty open about our opinions and feelings about relationships, sex, friendship, and pretty much any other subject. We eventually ended up sharing a double cubicle together. Since we really didn't see each other outside of work, most of our conversation happened while working. Tom was the one that I confided in after huge fights with Greg. He seemed to understand me and actually care about what I had to say.

Because we shared a cubicle, ours was larger than the standard 8-foot cube that single employees and contractors worked in. Connected to our cube was an 8-foot cubicle where an administrative "blue badge" sat. Her name was Davina. Davina was very nice, but if you spent more than 10 minutes in conversation with her, you would quickly realize how important her religion was to her. I was no stranger to this type of life, having grown up in such a strict religion myself. But since my divorce from Kyle, I'd become more of an open-minded, free thinker. This was exactly what my own religious upbringing warned against becoming, and although Davina was not a part of my childhood religion, she represented the thoughts and attitudes of all of the people I grew up with.

Even though I was a Christian and knew by this time that nothing would ever change that, there was something uncomfortable about being around extremely devout Christians who spoke out to everyone about their beliefs. I wasn't sure if the discomfort came from the feeling that I was being judged now that I had done so many things that were against my religious upbringing, or if it was because the religion of my childhood taught me that all other religions are false and to be strictly avoided. For lack of a better term, I was clearly "screwed up" when it came to religion. I didn't know for sure what I believed and preferred to acknowledge the things that I did not believe. One of the most important values I had learned so far since my divorce was the importance of the motto, "Live and Let Live." Having come this far in my life, it was very clear to me that you cannot judge another person without having lived through their experiences. I realized how difficult it was to manage my own life and make good decisions for myself and how pointless it was to worry about whether others were doing the right thing. But Davina was different, and when she spoke, she often made remarks as if to be "preaching." I was definitely not receptive to any type of preaching given my history, but trying to keep to my own "Live and Let Live" motto, I tried to shrug it off and realize that surely she meant well.

Sitting in the cubicle next to Davina had its downside as well, and Tom and I ended up being reprimanded on several occasions because Davina would overhear our conversation and become offended. The worst part was that she never approached Tom or me before going to management. Of course "reprimanded" meant that the boss, who happened to be a long time friend of several of the employees of Valeteka and who used to be a peer, would take you aside and say, "Hey, be careful what you say because Davina hears everything and has mentioned that some of the things she hears the two of you talk about are offensive." We decided that she probably really enjoyed hearing the conversations because even though we whispered, it was as if the quieter we spoke the more likely she was to hear. Truthfully, many of our conversations didn't belong at work, but we never spent time together outside of work and the controversial conversations between us were so much more fun than what I had to endure at home. The fighting with Greg seemed to get worse and worse and I often mentioned to Tom that I was going to leave eventually. Some days I'd show up at work and he could see the pain on my face from the previous night of crying. Lisa saw it too, and often reminded me that life was too short to stay in a bad relationship. I knew what I had to do, but actually doing it seemed so much harder.

It was almost the Fourth of July, and there was talk of a large group of Valeteka employees and a few blue badges that were getting together to go to Lake Tahoe to celebrate the holiday. One afternoon, when I was leaving work, Austin approached me in the hall. I had never talked to him before and we had only briefly been introduced on that first day of work, but I remembered him because he was the one that became a blue badge on the same day I started my job as an orange badge. He was walking towards me with a group of guys that I worked with and they were talking and laughing. Just before he reached me, the other guys took off in other directions as if they didn't want to be there when he spoke to me. He was my height, so our eyes made contact easily as he stopped in front of me. He seemed almost nervous when he spoke, but perhaps it was because his voice was soft.

"Hi Maddie, uhhh... I'm not sure if you heard that there is a group of people going to Lake Tahoe for the Fourth of July, and I wanted to let you know that you are invited if you'd like to come."

It was such a nice thought, a chance to get away from my stressful life and just be with a bunch of grownups, totally carefree for an entire weekend. No matter how exciting the weekend getaway sounded, I knew that it just wouldn't be the right thing to do. I would be putting myself in the wrong place at the wrong time.

I expressed my appreciation to Austin for the invitation and explained that I was going through a rough time in my marriage and that this was not the best time for me to run off on a fun-filled weekend. He seemed to understand and told me that if I changed my mind the invitation was open. I was usually pretty good at reading people, but I had a hard time reading him. I couldn't tell if one of the guys put him up to inviting me or if it was his idea. I couldn't tell if he was just inviting everyone, the more the merrier type of thing, or if he was interested in my company in particular. I wasn't sure how old he was, but he had graying hair and a goatee that was mostly dark with a silver streak down the left side. There was not a single line on his face, so the hair in itself was not enough to determine if he was significantly older than me. I didn't know much about him, but I had a feeling he was in a relationship with Kara, a woman who sat in a cube across the aisle from him. On occasion, I had to pass his cubicle to get to the printer, and I'd often see her giggling and chatting with him and they both seemed to not even notice that I would walk by, which made me feel that they were either interested in each other or seeing each other. A couple of weeks later, I heard that Kara was getting married. I didn't know whom she was marrying, but I figured it might be Austin. I knew that Tom was really good friends with Austin, but I wasn't really that interested, and so I never asked Tom about the two of them.

    With my new job and the kids visiting Kyle in Washington, the summer passed by quickly. It was hard knowing that my kids were spending time with Kyle's new wife as much or more than they were with Kyle. Especially knowing that whatever Kyle had told her about me had caused her to already dislike me. It was the first summer visitation for the kids and I missed them a lot. Greg and I took a trip to visit them for a weekend during their stay. It was a brief visit, and other than seeing the kids, it was nothing memorable.

    It was only about two months into my job with Valeteka when the kids had come home from Kyle's and were settled back into the school routine that I realized, or rather, finally admitted that I could no longer stay in a relationship with Greg and I had to let him know that I was leaving him. Greg took my announcement to leave surprisingly well. I am not sure if it was because deep down, he too was happy that the fighting would end, or if he truly believed that we would work things out and I would come back after some time to think. But I was never one to believe in trial separations. The notion sounded too much like practicing being apart, and we all know that practice makes perfect. The feeling of relief that I experienced after admitting that I could no longer stay with him was enough to recognize that I would not be repeating the same mistake twice. Even though I felt relief, there was a part of me that felt horribly guilty. I wondered if this must have been how Kyle felt when he admitted that he no longer loved me. I hated him so much for what he had done to me, and yet here I was feeling the same way towards Greg. Of course there was a certain amount of justification in the fact that I had only met Greg less than a year ago and married him on a rebound. It somehow didn't really compare to Kyle falling out of love with me after 12 years of marriage and three children together. I was worried about how the kids would take the news and about what type of lesson I was teaching them by blatantly disregarding the institution of marriage. I wasn't even sure what my own convictions were when it came to marriage. This once sacred union now seemed so easily dissolved that it felt more like a legal contract than anything hallowed. I waited until Greg wasn't home to talk to the kids because I wasn't sure what their reaction would be. I wanted them to be free to express themselves whether it was excitement or pain. Each of them reacted completely different than I expected, and as I suspected it was a good thing that Greg wasn't home. Kids have little tact and I'm sure that Greg wouldn't have taken it very well when he saw the expression on Levi's face as he jumped with excitement after hearing the news. He had to ask me a few times, "Are we really leaving?"

 Kaliegh was her usual self and was less expressive. She seemed to accept whatever the plan happened to be as if she was just along for the ride. But I will never forget the words that Katy spoke to me that afternoon. She looked me right in the eye and very softly she spoke as if she was the representative for the three of them.

 "Mom, we are not happy if you are not happy."

A NEW JOB

Until that moment, I had been living my life as if nothing I did really affected them. But it suddenly became very clear that even if they didn't seem to mind where we lived or whom I was married to, the bottom line was that they felt my pain and they felt my happiness. I had to start making decisions for the four of us and not just for myself.

I put a deposit down on a nearby apartment close to the kids' schools so I wouldn't have to move them again. The apartment wasn't ready, so I had to wait until it was available for move-in. Greg made it very easy to stay with him, although we were technically separated. Most of the time, he slept on the couch and stayed away from the house more than usual. We still had casual conversation, and there was a calmer side of Greg that I hadn't seen in a while. It was as if we were friends again. Perhaps it was never meant for us to take this relationship to the next level. I had hopes that we would remain friends after the marriage ended, but at the same time I was aware that all too often, it doesn't work out that way.

I spent most of my free time at home with the kids. One afternoon when we were all at home, the front door was opened and I heard Greg in the yard speaking to the neighbor next door. I went in the kitchen and looked outside and noticed that they were looking at an old car that Greg owned. The car had not been running for some time. I wasn't sure what the conversation was about, but I saw the woman hand Greg a small item. We had mostly been minding our own business during this separation phase and I wasn't going to start getting nosey now. I was looking forward to the future, and his conversations with neighbors didn't matter anymore. Even still, curiosity was natural and I was glad that Greg brought up the subject that evening.

We had been discussing our separation and who would take what. There wasn't much that we purchased together except for the washer and dryer, which I agreed to leave with him since my apartment included a set. Greg explained how the neighbor's eldest daughter had been having an affair with someone and now wanted to go back to her husband. She needed a car so that she could get a job. She wanted to get rid of a ring that was given to her by the guy she had a fling with because it reminded her of her mistake. She didn't have any money, so apparently she made a deal with Greg and part of the deal included the diamond ring in trade for the car. Greg pulled the small box out of his pocket.

"You should have this since I never bought you a wedding ring."

"Seriously?" I stared at the ring for a second or two; it was one single diamond in a simple gold band. It didn't look very expensive at first glance and I figured it probably wasn't since the neighbor readily gave it up in trade for the old car.

"I can't take this Greg, I mean now that we are splitting up it doesn't seem right."

He insisted that I take the ring; after all, he was keeping the washer and dryer. I thanked him and tucked the ring away in a drawer. I couldn't really wear it as a wedding ring now that our marriage was ending.

CHAPTER 18

A New Love

Going to work felt different now, knowing that my short marriage was actually ending. Nothing had changed except for the fact that I had told Greg that it was over and we were no longer sleeping in the same bed, but somehow I felt single. Even though in reality it would take some time for the paperwork to go through and the divorce to be final. There was a sense of freedom as I nurtured relationships at work with friends and co-workers and abandoned working on my relationship with Greg. It seemed strange to me that when we were trying to make things work we fought like crazy, and as soon as I announced that it was over the fighting had stopped as if there was no reason to agree on subjects anymore and hurtful words were pointless. Maybe those words were still spoken, but maybe now it didn't matter. After all, hurtful words only hurt you if you care. And I was only seeing the future, and that future didn't include Greg, at least not as a partner. Whether we could be friends was yet to be seen.

It was September and Lisa had recently introduced me to a friend of hers named Michelle. Michelle and I had a lot in common and Lisa was sure that we would hit it off. The three of us went wine tasting and Michelle and I became very close over the next few weeks. She lived in a neighborhood across the street from the apartment complex that I would be moving to, was married, and had a young daughter close to Levi's age. Even though she was married, she really seemed to understand what I was going through and we confided in each other about our relationship issues. One Friday evening we decided to go dancing. Although she wasn't planning a divorce and I could tell that she really loved her husband; I knew she was struggling with her relationship and we both felt that we needed to get out and have some fun. I arranged a sitter for the kids and I volunteered to be the designated driver. I knew I needed to keep a clear head if I wanted to stay out of trouble. I was vulnerable now that I wasn't sleeping with Greg and was on my way out the door when it came to our marriage.

We arrived at the club, and even though I wasn't new to the environment, it was different being there and not drinking. I considered myself a fun and outgoing person with or without alcohol, but in a sober state, I saw the entire club scene in a completely different light. I looked around the club and there was a good mix of people from various age groups. There were older men that seemed to be there just to watch. I made eye contact with one of them probably in his 50s, and he almost appeared to be bracing the wall so it didn't fall as he gripped his drink tightly in his hand. He smiled at me with his eyes, as he looked me up and down. There were younger guys on the dance floor with multiple women dancing around them.

Michelle quickly ordered a drink and we hit the dance floor right away. Dancing was one of my favorite things to do and I couldn't resist moving my body when the beat was good. We danced together as if we were friends to begin with, but after Michelle had a few more drinks, we were dancing like lesbians as we laughed. The guys around us could hardly keep their tongues in their mouths. At one point, I noticed a guy across the floor that couldn't stop staring at Michelle. I brought it to her attention and in her inebriated state she insisted that since she was married and couldn't make a move on him, that I must go across the room and kiss him and let her know how it was.

A NEW LOVE

With alcohol in my system that would have been an easy task because I'd likely act on impulse and think about it later. But being totally sober, it was a little trickier. I actually had to make a decision, consider all consequences, and act on whatever that decision was. It was so much more complicated. I think for the first time, I really needed a drink. I thought about it as she persisted. Finally, I decided it didn't matter, why not? I was closer to single than she was, and honestly, I was bored with the whole club scene, my feet were tired of dancing, and most importantly, I was curious. I was more curious about what kind of response I would get than I was about his ability to kiss. He was very sexy, so that made the task a little more appealing. I made eye contact with him and began to make my way across the crowded dance floor in his direction. My heart was pounding and I almost turned around and went back to Michelle, but before I had a chance, I was standing right in front of him. I smiled and flirtatiously explained how my poor friend across the room was already married and since I was unattached she wanted me to find out how good of a kisser he was. He looked her direction and she smiled and waved like a little girl as she moved to the music. Michelle was a gorgeous brunette and he was obviously attracted to her, which made his reaction even more interesting. He smiled and waved at her and then without hesitation he slipped a hand around my waste and bent down to reach me, and planted a deep and sexy kiss on my lips. My heart raced. I wasn't sure if it was because he was a good kisser or if it was in the anticipation and excitement of kissing a total stranger. I never even asked him his name. I simply said thanks and turned around and went back to Michelle. She was shocked that I actually did it and insisted that I tell her how he kissed. I wasn't sure how to explain a kiss. And now that the excitement was over, I wasn't sure if it was the greatest kiss after all but didn't want to let her down, so I proceeded to define the kiss as an extremely sensual and intoxicating one.

We danced until our feet were killing us. At one point a bunch of guys attending a bachelor party begged us to leave with them in a rented bus that was barhopping around town. I had to convince Michelle that it wouldn't be a wise thing to do. The evening was great and I was happy that Michelle was in my life. Michelle and Lisa were the only female friends I really had now that my relationship was over. Kyle was my best friend from the time I was 15. Until meeting Michelle, I wasn't sure if I was capable of being best friends with a woman. But Michelle put her all into her friendships and I knew that I could count on her to be there if I needed her.

My apartment move-in date was fast approaching and I spent my after work hours for the next week or so packing up boxes. By now, everyone at work knew my circumstances, and just like after my separation from Kyle, there seemed to be a sudden jump in the number of interested men. I often wondered if men really were that perceptive and that as soon as they found out I was single they really came around more often, or if it was more a case of my own awareness that there was no longer going to be a man in my life, which caused me to open up my eyes and notice the men that were there all along. In either case, they were there. I started to look around me and when I would talk to single men, I'd ask myself if this was the next potential relationship. I knew it would probably be good for me to concentrate on my kids and do nothing more than look at the opposite sex for a while. But I knew from experience that being single and lonely, all it would take for me to give in to my sexual desires would be for me to be alone with a man I was attracted to and for him to make the first move. For now I was safe, because the only man I was alone with was Greg, and that relationship was over. I guess the stress of my ending relationship, moving, and my new job was starting to show on my face because Tom seemed to notice.

"Maddie, you really need to get out of the house some."

He was right. I had been unable to go out with Michelle and every spare moment had been spent making arrangements, pack-

A NEW LOVE

ing, or basically on some other obligation. I was starting to get depressed, and if Tom was noticing, then surely my kids could feel it too.

"Any suggestions Tom?"

"Yes! There is a whole group getting together to go to the best pizza place in California on Friday night. It's an hour drive or so, but worth every mile."

I wasn't much of a pizza person to start with, and I couldn't imagine liking it enough to drive an hour for it. Tom offered to give me a ride with him and his girlfriend, and I really wanted to go. I didn't know everyone that would be there, but it didn't really matter because anything was better than another weekend of packing and organizing. So I made arrangements for an all-night sitter and accepted the invite. I felt like I'd be a third wheel, but Tom insisted it was no big deal and that his girlfriend Lacey would be fine with it. The rest of the week seemed to crawl by, probably because I was so looking forward to an evening with other adults.

When Friday evening finally arrived, I was totally ready, and Tom and Lacey arrived at my house as planned. The ride was long, but seemed to go by quick with the three of us talking the whole way. We finally arrived at the famous "Frank's Pizza." Tom had mentioned this place on previous occasions and apparently it was a long-time hang-out for him and his friends. The place looked small from the outside, and when we entered and saw how small it was on the inside, I was sure our group would end up taking up the whole place. We were early, so Tom ordered a pitcher of beer. I had never been a beer person, but Tom said the beer was on him and so I drank. I rarely drank with a purpose, but this night was different. I needed to relax. Everything was so serious in my life; divorce, parenting, moving, it was all taking its toll on my normally bubbly personality. I knew it would only take a glass of beer to get the job done. But what I didn't anticipate was Tom topping off my glass. I'm sure he thought he was doing me a favor. He knew how stressed out I'd been and wanted to see me have fun.

It wasn't long before the rest of the group started showing up. A handful of Tom's male friends showed up first, and then Austin arrived with a couple of friends and another blue badge from work. Her name was Amber. She was very pretty and I was aware of the many rumors about her and her habit of sleeping with coworkers, and as rumor had it, sometimes managers. Even though it was hearsay, my objectivity was compromised by the unsubstantiated rumors. At the same time, I was no one to judge. Maybe I'd not been sleeping with current coworkers, but I had my share of sleeping with strangers, friends, and Blake, who was my coworker in Texas. At previous jobs, I would hear rumors about a woman sleeping around from other women. This time, I was hearing the rumors from the male perspective. The interesting part is that the men seemed just as disgusted as the women, yet most of them were more than willing to be her next victim. The rumors were that she didn't care if the guy was already in a relationship or even married. I had often heard of women like this referred to as "home-wreckers," but after my break up with Kyle, I saw it differently. If a man wants to cheat on his wife, he will find a willing woman. My thoughts are that the responsibility lies on the married person to reject the advances of the so-called "home-wrecker." And if he doesn't, then she merely set the stage and he is the actual home-wrecker.

I had already had a few glasses of beer when the rest of the group arrived. We shuffled tables around trying to get as many people gathered into the already tiny dining area as we could. I changed seats multiple times as people arrived. As Austin tossed his jacket over a chair, I decided to take the chair next to him, but Amber was quicker than me. I was really feeling the alcohol by then. A friend from work, Donna, arrived about that time, so I asked her to sit on one side of me and Tom to sit on the other side, jokingly commenting that one of them could keep me off

A NEW LOVE

the table and the other could keep me off the floor. There was a ton of conversation going on at one time, and before long, the alcohol had totally taken over and I was walking around the table measuring the size of the guys hands to see who had the largest sexual anatomy. This is exactly the reason I should have known better than to hang out after hours with people I work with. But for the time being, I didn't care about how I would face any of them in the days to come. At one point, as I was busy being silly, I stood up to reach across the table and felt a slap on my butt. I was wearing very short shorts, so I was probably asking for trouble in the first place. I turned around and saw Austin, who had managed to drag his chair down to my end of the table and to squeeze in between Donna and I.

"Hey, did you just slap my ass?"

"Uhh, yeah!" He looked like he wasn't sure what to expect. "I've been trying to get your attention so I could talk to you."

I sat down as he proceeded to ask me all kinds of questions. I did my best to answer them, being that I was totally drunk by this time. I especially remember thinking about how I had never really noticed him before. Even if I had noticed him, I wasn't quite yet available and so everyone was just slightly off limits. But now, he had definitely gotten my attention and we talked non-stop for the rest of the evening. I learned that he was indeed single and the flirting with his neighboring cube dweller was nothing more than flirting. Other than that detail, I honestly don't remember the things we must have talked about, but the gist of the conversation was his wanting to know all about me. One thing I had learned about alcohol is that it caused me to be totally honest, sometimes painfully so. And when it was time to leave, I didn't want to end my conversation with him. I grabbed his hand and told him he was coming with me. And to my surprise, as I drug him out the door, he followed, and as we left he yelled to Amber and the group that he arrived with that he was catching a ride with Tom. We climbed in the back seat of Tom's car. I scooted as close to

Austin as possible. My head was spinning and the beer seemed to have a different effect on me than mixed drinks or wine.

As Tom drove out of the parking lot, I looked into Austin's eyes. For a moment it was as if we were all alone even though Tom and Lacey were just in the front seat. I turned towards him and pressed my body against his. I remember the pounding of my heart and the scent of his skin. Normally the alcohol had a tendency to numb my senses, but tonight they were sharper than ever. He leaned towards me, took my bottom lip into his mouth and tenderly kissed me. As our lips touched ever so gently over and over again, I felt a rush of heat go through my body. He placed his hand on the side of my neck as if to hold my head steady as he continued to kiss me. His lips were soft and each time they touched mine it was sweet and tender. His goatee was soft against my face, and everything about him felt right. And then the effects of the alcohol hit me. I was experiencing something different than I had experienced before.

I suddenly felt overwhelmingly sad. It probably didn't help that I had accepted this invitation because I'd been feeling down, and then I overdid it with the intake of alcohol and now my body was feeling its effects. I started to cry, which must have taken Austin by surprise. I remember pouring my heart out about how all I really wanted was to be happy. Tears ran down my cheeks and we alternated between my crying and pouring out my feelings and deep passionate kissing. Looking back, I wonder how Tom and Lacey kept a straight face all the way home with an hour of my tears and pain and making out with Austin in their back seat. Surely I would regret this night later. Austin's house was on the way to mine, so Tom dropped him off first. I remember that Austin's roommate was standing in the lawn with a group of guys that I recognized from work. Everything was starting to go fuzzy, but my tears were gone and were replaced once again with silly laughter. Tom rolled his back window down and I remember one of the guys putting his hand in the back window. I grabbed two fingers and put them in my mouth and then I let them slowly slide out from between my lips. There was a lot of laughter and talking going on, and I was quickly fading. Before long, I was being dropped off in front of my house, or what was actually Greg's house. I was moving the next day and this was no time for me to be drunk. I stumbled into the house and Greg was still awake. It was obvious that I'd been drinking, but Greg didn't seem to care. I think he had accepted that I was leaving and he didn't really ask any questions, maybe because he didn't really want to hear the answers.

The following morning, I woke with a painful headache. I had to pick the kids up in the afternoon, but first I had to face the reality of what had happened the night before. I sat up in my bed in a cold sweat. Could this all have been a dream? I knew it wasn't. What would I do? I had to go back to work in two days and I had just spent approximately seven hours making a fool out of myself in front of people that I had to work with on a daily basis. I couldn't just show up at work on Monday morning. I had to at least talk to Austin before then. I didn't even have his number and had no idea how to contact him. I quickly remembered that I had a phone list on my badge. I thought maybe his name was still on the back of the badge with the list of other coworkers. I scrambled out of bed to find it. His name was not on the back. So I called a couple other numbers on the back of the badge hoping that someone had his number, and after calling a few people who didn't have it, I finally found someone who did. He explained that he wasn't supposed to just give out personal numbers unless I had a business need. I was sure he was messing with me. What harm could there be in giving me Austin's number? I made up some story about how I needed boxes and Austin said he had some that I could have, so he gave me the number. I was pretty sure he knew that I was full of crap and that there was something going on between us. I didn't even think about what I would say before I picked up the phone to call him. When he answered, the first thing that came to my mind was the story I had just made up about boxes, so I asked him if by any chance he had a few boxes for the final packing I had to do. He stammered around a bit.

"Umm, well, sure, yeah, I have a few."

"So are you going to be home for a while, do you think I could come get them?"

"Umm... Yeah... I'm leaving in a couple of hours, but I'll be here until then. You can come by if you want."

He gave me his address and directions to his house, since there was no way I could recall how to get there from the previous evening.

"Ok, great! Thanks... See you in a bit."

I jumped out of bed and took a five minute shower, ran a blow dryer through my hair, rushed to put my makeup on, slipped on my tight pair of jeans and a low-cut t-shirt, grabbed my keys, and ran out the door. It took roughly 20 minutes to get to his house, but it felt like only a matter of seconds. My mind was racing and I wasn't totally sure what I was even going to say; I only knew that I had to talk to him about what happened the night before.

When I arrived, the garage door was open. I parked on the street in front of the house and walked up to the garage, where Austin's roommate Jake greeted me. I knew Jake already from Valateka.

"Hi Jake, is Austin home?"

"Yeah he's in the house... Let me go get him."

He went back inside the house and I looked around the garage, but didn't see any boxes. I didn't really need boxes since I was totally packed up and had plans to move into the apartment that weekend. I wondered if he even had boxes to give me or if he too was making up a story to get me to come over. After a minute, Austin came out of the house. It was an awkward moment.

I slipped my hands in the front pockets of my tight jeans and tried to make eye contact. I'm sure my face was a bright shade of blushing red. He appeared to be just as uncomfortable as I was.

"Hi Austin... Umm, I know I said I needed boxes, but I guess I really just needed to talk to you."

"Yeah... Well, honestly, I don't have any boxes anyway; I just wanted to see you."

"You know I wasn't really myself last night. Beer is just not my drink and I can't really handle much alcohol anyway, so I'm afraid by the time you showed up at Frank's, I was already out of control."

"I understand, really."

"Well... I figured it would be very awkward if we just ran into each other at work without discussing what happened last night. And even though I was totally wasted, I really enjoyed kissing you."

He had a warm, natural, olive glow to his skin and now he was blushing as well.

"I really enjoyed it too, and I enjoyed our conversation."

"Yeah... Well I'm really sorry about the crying and whining about how my life totally sucks. It's really not that bad; I think it was the alcohol talking."

"I get it. That's expected when you drink. No biggy."

"So, maybe we can get together for lunch next week?"

I wasn't sure why I was extending the invitation to lunch. I knew I liked him, but I also already swore to myself that I'd stay away from men for a while. I mean, I wasn't even moved out of my house yet and I was already getting myself into trouble. Austin agreed to lunch and we set a date for Wednesday.

The rest of the weekend was crazy and moving with three kids proved to be a daunting task. Greg had a few of his friends help move the big furniture and we crammed all three kids' belongings into the master bedroom of the apartment complex. I took the smaller bedroom for myself. The space was tight, but sufficient for the four of us. I put myself on a waiting list for a three-bedroom unit, but I was informed that it could take up to a year to get one. It would be hard for the girls to share with Levi, but he was still little so we just threw a small mattress under the bottom bunk bed and turned it into a makeshift trundle. Greg and I were getting along well for the time being. I believe that he felt we'd get back together. At this point I wasn't sure about anything, but I hoped that we could at least maintain a friendship. I was pretty sure that as soon as I had a boyfriend, Greg would disappear from my life. The fact that I already visualized myself in another relationship did not surprise me. I knew that deep down I was the married type. The thought of being alone was terrifying, and as long as there was a potential to find a compatible mate, I would be looking for that one special person to spend the rest of my life with.

Monday morning was awkward. I had to face Tom, and as expected, he gave me hell for the Austin make-out session on the way home from Frank's. I deserved every bit of the teasing that I got, as well as the stares from the rest of the guys that showed up and heard all the stories. I was pretty sure Austin wasn't sharing details with the rest of the group, but I remembered that I had put someone's fingers in my mouth, and as disgusting as the thought was after the fact, it happened, and whoever he was had to be sharing all the details and possibly fabricating a few along the way. Neither Austin nor I went out of our way to see each other. In fact, it almost seemed as if we were avoiding contact. When I thought about what happened, I felt a flutter in my chest and a little weak at the knees. Blake was the last person that made me feel that way and I definitely wanted to see Austin again, but there was a lot of awkwardness about seeing him. It wasn't like we met, then dated, then kissed. There was no proper order to our relationship, if you could even call it that. That night was more happenstance than anything else.

By Wednesday, we had to speak because we had plans to have lunch together at a nearby Italian restaurant. We agreed to take separate cars. I would have been happy to ride with him had he offered, but it was his idea to meet there. We showed up about the same time and parked right next to each other. When we went to be seated, he asked the hostess for a booth in the back and throughout our lunch, I could tell that he was looking around to make sure that there was no one he recognized. When I asked him if he was afraid to be seen with me, he said he just didn't want any rumors to get started that we were dating or anything. I had to remind him that the rumors had already started. Other than his nervousness, our conversation was lively and being with him felt natural. I decided that I had to pay for lunch since I extended the invitation. To my embarrassment, my card was declined. I knew it was a system error. I had plenty of money in the bank, but my debit card was brand new so it must not have been activated properly. I tried explaining, but it sounded like an excuse and I was just making myself look worse. I was so glad he had the ability to pay and we joked about how if he hadn't, we'd be doing dishes for the rest of the afternoon.

After lunch, we walked back to his truck, and as soon as I had the opportunity, I leaned in to kiss him goodbye. After all, I had kissed him for the long ride home from Frank's, so I figured I might as well see if he was receptive in a sober state. The kiss was strange, and he was obviously holding back. I could feel how tense he was, and once again, he seemed to be looking around to make sure no one else saw us. I laughed, and instead of being offended, I was actually attracted to his quiet shyness. I wasn't used to that type of guy and his non-aggressiveness was appealing. I wanted to make plans to see him again, but I could tell I was being pushy enough and was afraid I would scare him away if I asked too soon. So instead, I asked him if I could call him sometime and his response was, "Absolutely." He seemed very sincere and I was glad. I was beginning to worry that the whole experience was just a drunken mistake in his eyes. But it would have been just as easy to say no to my lunch invitation or even easier to make up some "I'm too busy" excuse.

I decided that although I would pursue his company, it was best to lay low at work until we got to know each other better. Mostly for his sake, since he seemed to be uneasy about what other people would think. While I drove away, I thought about how far I'd come since Kyle and I first split up. Here I was making the moves, when up until now I was the one being hit on. So far things seemed to just happen to me, but finally I was planning what would happen next. It felt good to have the confidence and to be the one in control of my future.

I called Austin that night after the kids were asleep and we talked for hours. We talked on the phone every night that week and even stayed on the phone until 4 a.m. when we had to go to work at 7 a.m. the next morning. We were both exhausted at work, and when people asked, I blamed it on the move and being a single parent again. We seemed to have so much in common and it was so easy to talk to him. And then there was my whole life story, which would take many hours to explain to him. I was amazed by how much time went into establishing a relationship. Even though I enjoyed talking to him, sometimes hashing up things that had happened to me in the last year was painful. He had his share of painful stories from his past as well. He had been engaged once before and the relationship ended when he found out she had been cheating on him. Still, he was so different than me. He was 30 years old and had never been married or had children. I was only three months younger than him and yet had experienced almost 13 years of marriage, two husbands, and three children. As much as I was drawn to him and even though the physical attraction was there, I still told myself that he was off limits for any permanent relationship. I couldn't see how he or any man could become and instant father to three kids and how any marriage could survive the baggage that comes along with two ex-husbands. There were so many issues between Kyle and I, and it seemed as though they would never go away. From child support disagreements to visitation arrangements to the unending bitterness that grew between us. If my divorce had been like my sister's, where Kyle and I got along for the sake of the kids and where we could at least be civil towards one another, then perhaps things would be different. I felt that any permanent relation-

A NEW LOVE

ship in the future would only be successful if I could find a man who had gone through similar things as I had.

On Friday night after the kids had gone to sleep, I curled up on my bed with my cordless phone, as I had done every other night that week, and called Austin. We had talked so many hours about everything under the sun and I had enjoyed every conversation, but tonight was different. I longed to see his facial expressions when he spoke. We were getting to know each other and the phone seemed cold, and even though he lived only 15 minutes from me, there was a feeling of much greater distance when we spoke. I was lonely for physical contact and I knew that he was too. But with three kids at home, there was no time for going out. I'd have to have a sitter, and with one income, that was more than my budget allowed. I felt that the only time I would ever get to spend with him would be at work or on the phone. This particular night our conversation turned more intimate. We talked about sex and our feelings about the fact that I was legally still married, but physically separated and filing for divorce. And then, we started talking about that night at Frank's and how much sexual attraction was between us. Before long, I was inviting him over. It was 2 a.m., so he would have to sneak and be very quiet so he wouldn't wake up the kids. I didn't want them to know anything about my personal relationships and had no intentions of introducing them to any man unless I could see that it would be a potentially permanent relationship. And on this particular night, there was no thought of permanence. The only thing I was thinking about was my physical desire to be with him. I wasn't sure how he'd react, since so far any talk of a sexual nature had been initiated by me and although it was obvious he was attracted to me, I wasn't sure how he felt about taking it to the next level. But up until that point, my experience, although limited, had proven that if offered an opportunity for sex with an attractive woman, a man would not turn it down. And this time was no different.

Austin quietly accepted and we hung up the phone. My heart

was pounding. I had been drinking wine during our phone conversation. I hadn't even bothered with a wine glass. It was just as tasty and relaxing right out of the bottle. By this time, clearly my inhibitions had been limited. But now, I had already extended the invitation and the inevitable was going to happen. I'd been in bed in my frumpy PJs, so I quickly jumped out of bed, pulled open a dresser drawer, and sifted through the lingerie that I had accumulated over the years. I found a slinky, red nightie that was sexy, but not too risqué. I took off my PJs and slipped the satin fabric over my shoulders. I caught a glimpse of my reflection in the mirror and felt confident that this was the best one for the first impression. I lit a few candles and put on some soft music. I grabbed my robe and turned out the light. I had to wait in the living room so he wouldn't have to knock and risk waking up the kids. I knew he was headed straight over and I had very little time to think about my decision.

With the wine and the memory of the passionate kisses we had shared, there was no room for guilt. Yet still, I was nervous. Even though it was a spontaneous decision, it was more planned than the previous "first times" that I had experienced. After about 20 minutes I could hear his footsteps coming up the stairs. My heart pounded with anticipation. I looked through the peephole and as soon as he approached the door I started to unlock the chain and deadbolt so he would hear me and not knock. I opened the door with one hand, still clutching the bottle of wine in the other. Austin looked just as nervous as I did. I anxiously let him in and was eager to get him in my bedroom just in case the kids woke up. We were whispering and tiptoeing back to my room. I imagined that had I been a naughty teenager, this is what it would feel like to sneak in a teenage boy in the middle of the night. The sneaking actually added to the excitement.

As soon as we entered my bedroom, I turned around and closed the door behind us and then turned back around towards Austin. I placed the bottle of wine on the dresser beside me and I untied my robe and dropped it to the floor to reveal the sheer negligee underneath. We had spent so many hours in conversation and I was wasting no time. The physical chemistry was strong and I wanted to feel my body next to his. He pulled his shirt off over his shoulders and carefully laid it across the foot of my bed. I took a moment to examine his muscular shoulders as the candlelight bounced across his body. Neither of us said a word as he reached forward and slipped the straps of my negligee off my shoulders. He moved closer to me and looked me in the eye for a moment before leaning to my ear and whispering the words, "You are beautiful." He gently kissed my neck and then took the sides of my face into his hands and kissed me tenderly on the lips. I placed my hands on his shoulders and nudged him towards my bed. Hardly another word was exchanged as we explored each other passionately. But there was something different about this experience. It seemed more intimate than purely sexual. There was a sense of seriousness to Austin and a tender, soft side that left me feeling as though he genuinely cared about me. Maybe because of the many conversations that we had shared, we had built a sort of warm friendship which had ignited different feelings that your typical raw sexual appetite.

He spent several hours with me as I lay in his arms and we whispered softly to make sure we didn't wake the kids. But before daylight, he left as quietly as he had arrived. I lay in my bed alone; I knew that I wanted to see him again and the thought actually scared me. I had already ruled him out as a lifetime partner. There were too many things he didn't have experience with. I was sure I'd have to find someone who had been divorced and had at least had one child. Austin wasn't that man. I felt that he deserved to find someone who had a similar situation as he did, someone that he could have children with who could share the "first time" experiences with him. It was then that I realized that I'd have to make it perfectly clear to him that while I wanted to spend time with him, I didn't want him to fall in love with me. I wanted to enjoy our time together, but wanted him to keep his options open, and if and when he or I found a more suitable partner, that we would go our separate ways. So the very next time we talked, I made sure he understood our relationship. I didn't want to be responsible for hurting him. He seemed fine with the arrangement and we continued the sneak in and sneak out routine for the next several weeks. He didn't seem as careful about people knowing we were together, and by now everyone at work was aware that we were seeing each other. We didn't label it as dating or boyfriend and girlfriend; it was just seeing each other.

Financially things were still very difficult for me. Although my income was good for a single person, it was difficult making ends meet for a family of four. Child support helped but I found myself living paycheck to paycheck. Being a single mother had its challenges. I rarely got sick myself but when one of the kids was sick I'd have to stay home from work. On one such occasion, Levi had a fever and I called in to use one of my sick days. Somehow I'd overlooked the company policy that if you call in sick the day before a holiday you would lose your holiday pay for that day. Since every dollar was spent before I received my paycheck I was devastated when I found that my check less than usual. When Austin found out he tried to give me money but I refused. He insisted that it would be a loan but I wasn't willing to have money come between us. I wanted to be able to cut ties at anytime and for him to have the same freedom. Owing him money would make things more complicated. I was desperate and told him about my plan to go to the pawnshop and sell the diamond ring that Greg had given me. Austin wouldn't let me and he insisted that he wanted to buy the ring. It seemed like a good idea since he offered $200, which was more than the pawnshop would give me. By this time, Greg had chosen to be out of my life completely and since there was no sentimental connection to the ring and I hadn't had it appraised, having the money to pay my bills was my first priority. The money allowed me to catch up and prevented me from paying outrageous interest on a payday cash advance from a quick cash establishment.

A NEW LOVE

It was almost Halloween when Austin invited me to a party at his house. I eagerly accepted and although people knew we were seeing each other, this would be our first opportunity to be together as a couple around a large group of his friends. He decided to be some kind of wolf; I decided to be a sexy dominatrix. With my bills paid and a few dollars left over I went shopping at a nearby lingerie shop that had a specialty section for strippers. I found a skintight pair of shiny leggings that were missing a section in the thigh area, and the top and bottom parts were connected with silver chains. I found a black leather bra with silver metal studs and a skimpy sleeveless leather jacket that exposed part of the bra in the front. Then I found a studded choker, a pair of knee high stiletto boots, some chains to hang on my jacket, handcuffs, and a whip. I didn't have a lot of money and so I always tried to get a deal from small local shops. The guy that worked at the shop offered to give me 70% off if I would promise to come by the store and let him take my picture on the way to the party. I never asked for these types of deals, but it seemed that they were always there. I figured it was because I was such an outgoing person that people were not afraid to approach me. Who knows what he wanted to do with the picture but I needed to save money so I agreed.

The week before the party was my quarterly evaluation and I had a meeting set up with my boss. This was not the boss who hired me. There had been several changes in command and my new boss was a good friend of Austin's. In fact, most of the employees that worked in our building were a pretty close bunch and they not only worked together, but they also played together. Some of them had worked together for many years. It was obvious that Austin had a lot of friends, yet I was still shocked by the warning from my new boss. Halfway through my evaluation, he warned me that he was going "off the record." Then he proceeded to tell me how Austin was a good friend of his, as well as many others that worked there, and he explained that he wanted to make very sure that Austin was not getting played because there would be a lot of angry people if he got hurt. I wasn't surprised that Austin had such loyal friends. He was so easy going and fun to be with and I didn't know anyone who didn't like him. But now I almost felt guilty. Of course his warning didn't change my plans. There was no "being played" involved. I had made it very clear to Austin that I was just having fun and there was no potential of the two of us becoming involved in any long-term relationship, other than possibly friends. Although I didn't feel it was my boss's place on or off the record to warn me about how to proceed with my personal relationships, I had to play it safe because this early into the job I wasn't sure just how far he might take the warning and I couldn't afford to lose my job. I assured him that I was not playing games and that Austin was a big boy and could take care of himself.

Even still, I was aware that I was being watched and I worried that when the time came for Austin and I to break up that I might actually have to quit my job just to avoid the wrath of his friends. But as time passed, I never felt the need to break up with him. I went to Austin's Halloween party, and against my initial decision, I introduced him to my kids, and we all began to build a very special bond. It became very evident to me how strong my feelings for him had grown during one particular conversation we had before going to a party. While I don't remember where we were going, I remember specifically the conversation. Austin was merely following the rules that I had set.

"Who knows, when we get there, maybe I'll meet someone or you'll meet someone and we can go our separate ways."

At that moment, I felt a sharp shooting pain go through my chest. I had gotten so used to our flirting at work, and going to lunch together every day, and talking on the phone for hours, and him sneaking in my bedroom at night, that I had forgotten that by my own admission, he would not be "the one" I ended up with. I knew exactly what the pain in my chest meant. I was getting attached. I was doing exactly what I ordered him not to do. I was falling in love. I knew my only choice was to break up right then and there before my feelings got any stronger and caused more pain when it finally ended. But Austin wouldn't let me end the relationship. He insisted that although he wasn't sure if what he felt for me was love, he was sure that he'd never been happier and that he'd never wanted to be with anyone else as much as he wanted to be with me. Somehow, he convinced me to stick it out. I guess the pain of breaking up was already difficult, so it was either I feel the pain right then or later. I decided to stay until he was ready to go his own way. It was only a week or two later that I was sure that I was in love. By then, there was no way I was going to break up with him. Yet still, I expected that the break up was inevitable and that I would just enjoy whatever time I had with him.

We spent all of our free time together; he had Thanksgiving dinner with us and we spent Christmas together as well. There was something special about our relationship. I remember how I would get into a deep dialog about some totally unnecessary subject and he would stop me mid conversation just to tell me, "I like the way you think." I was used to men who told me I thought too much. He was like a breath of fresh air. I would find myself apologizing for things that I would do that used to irritate Kyle. Austin would look at me and ask, "Why are you sorry?" I had never felt so accepted. We often talked about what a relationship meant to each of us. I had been through so much and although knowing exactly what I wanted was difficult, it was simple to figure out what I didn't want. The main thing I wanted to avoid was fighting. There was so much screaming and yelling in my relationship with Kyle that I promised I would be history at the first sign of a heated argument. But communication between us was effortless. Austin was so easygoing that I often wondered if he was acting. But there was no way he could keep up an act like that. I finally decided he truly was amazing.

After Christmas, he was going to take a trip to New Zealand to visit family. A few nights before he left, as I lay in his arms telling him how much I was going to miss him while he was away, he softly whispered the words, "I love you." I wasn't sure if I had heard him correctly and so I looked at him and he repeated those three little words, "I love you." This was the first time in my life that I felt what it was like to experience true "grown-up" love. This love was so different than the love I had for Kyle. I had loved Kyle; after all, we had been together since I was 15. But falling in love as an adult was a completely different experience. If you had asked me when I was 15 why I loved Kyle, I wouldn't have known what to say. But there were not enough words to express my feelings of love for Austin. I wasn't supposed to fall in love with him and he was not supposed to fall in love with me. So there we were - two people that weren't supposed to be. But as I lay there in his arms, there was something comfortable, something right about being with him. And in that moment I felt as if all the stars had come into alignment and I had found my match made in heaven. While he was away, I spent all my free time painting his portrait, which for an artist is a sign of true love.

CHAPTER **19**

Beyond The Present

Austin and I dated for approximately 8 months before we decided to purchase a house together. Buying a house was a big step because I'd actually be living with a man without being married. I knew that my decision would play a significant role in shaping my children's ideals of marriage and relationships. But I had jumped into marriage twice in my life already. We talked about marriage and we both knew that it was the ultimate goal, but we weren't in a hurry. I figured that we'd live together for a couple of years and then we'd get married. But one night, not long after moving in to our new house, he proposed as we lay on the living room floor. His proposal was unique. He told me he wanted to marry me and he wanted to have kids. I wasn't surprised that he wanted children. From the beginning of our relationship, he told me that he loved the relationship I had with my kids. We had talked about whether I'd be willing to have more children. There was no question in my mind by now as to whether Austin would be a good husband and father. I was totally head over heals in love and I accepted without hesitation.

Ironically the diamond that I had sold to him when I was desperate for cash to pay my bills ended up being the center stone for my engagement ring. I sold it to him for a mere $200 and once the ring appraised we learned that it was a nearly colorless and flawless diamond worth over $5000. I often joke about how the only way I could get my diamond back was to marry him.

We were married only four months after our engagement on Dec 5, 1998. Eleven years later, Austin is still my best friend and my match made in heaven. Our relationship is built on mutual respect and trust. There is no yelling or screaming between us. We share everything and support each other through rain or shine. We have two beautiful baby girls together and all three of my children with Kyle call him Dad. They have two dads now. Katy is soon to graduate from college as a high school history teacher and recently walked down the aisle with Kyle on one side and Austin on the other and married the man of her dreams. Kaliegh has found true love and is engaged. She has recently graduated summa cum laude with a Bachelor's of Arts Degree in Psychology. Levi is graduating from high school and has a promising future following his love for journalism.

I often worried that my failed marriages and touch and go relationships would affect my children's ability to develop relationships of their own. But now that I see them and how happy they are, perhaps my experiences and my ability to find Austin, as well as seeing the healthy relationship that we have, has offered them a chance to recognize that true love is worth seeking.

It is hard to remember the sadness and the pain that I endured with so much joy and happiness in my life today. But I do remember people telling me that I'd look back one day and the pain would be just a faded memory. Sometimes, when you are experiencing the down times that naturally go along with living, it's hard to believe it will ever get better. Although I've put the past behind me, it is still an intricate part of who I am. Perhaps I made many mistakes along the way, but I prefer to call them learning experiences. Although I have learned many lessons from my experiences, the single most valuable lesson involved endurance. No matter how bad things get or how hopeless life seems I've learned to always look beyond the present.

CPSIA information can be obtained
at www.ICGtesting.com
Printed in the USA
FSHW020431030222
88099FS

9 781432 754754